THE KINGDOM MINDSET OF WORK

AN EVERY BELIEVER, EVERYDAY KINGDOM MANUAL

A USEFUL TOOL FOR EFFECTIVE END-TIME MINISTRY

Creative Ministry Resources Publishing Email: creativeministry_music@gmail.com

Hardcover ISBN 978-976-96137-2-0

Paperback ISBN 978-976-96137-3-7

Ebook ISBN 978-976-96137-4-4

INDEX

INTRODUCTION

THE ASSIGNMENT

The sun took an intimate inspection of the landscape and kissed it goodbye with an ever so warm and extended kiss as it slowly rode away into the dusk. It was a leisurely and passionate departure that culminated in the warmest of sunsets as if to say, "Every minute spent with you is a moment to treasure; it is very important to me. I want you to remember me with this colorful, blushing smile."

The minister was in his final days. He knew he would be departing from this life soon. Like the sun he had a full day. He smiled as he considered the millions he had reached in his lifetime, the many institutions he had impacted and the many sons he had raised up who were currently on fire for the Lord. Unlike the sun he would not be returning to time. He would never get the opportunity to do so again. He however had the opportunity to leave himself behind.

"I will be going to meet the Son, soon," he smiled to himself. "The real Son that puts light in this life that never goes out. The Son in me that is burning hotter than ever now that I am so close. But I am not ready yet, there is one thing He desires of me before I leave. I must deposit my heart to my successor. He already has a heart for ministry. He is very intelligent and full of the Spirit. Effectiveness however is hinged on one principle that believers generally ignore, the principle of work. I have trained him well but I need him to get this one key aspect that differentiates between success and real success. It is one key that if not embraced, results in many souls being lost in everyday believer's casual walk and course of life."

The sun going down had a particular significance for him. His son would be with him very soon. Each day he looked forward to the sun going down because it was so beautiful and so deliberate. He had a superb view of it as it danced in the valley just outside his window. He also knew that when it left, he would see his son by natural and spiritual birth, his successor, coming in. This meant everything to him in these final hours.

The doctors had given him five (5) days to live. He was willing to let go but not yet. He had already gone nine days and he knew he needed another two weeks to get this message across in the way he wanted to. He felt the peace in his heart that told him he would have the time. This is a message his son needed, the church needed; all believers needed this message to fully represent the Lord Jesus in these end times.

He smiled as the door turned and the face of his son burst through. His personal nurse left his bedside and went out as he embraced the moment.

After the regular emotional greetings, He asked his son, "John, what have you discovered?"

He had given him an assignment two days before that involved research, meditation and prayerful contemplation.

He was very anxious to hear his response.

"Father, I have never seen it this way before," John gushed.

PRIESTHOOD

A CALL TO WORK

John began to relate to His father his revelations: "Daddy, the priests of old exhausted themselves with fixed routines and arduous duties to minister to, intercede for, and represent the people to God and God to the people. This duty of presenting God to man is nothing but hard work."
His father smiled and responded, "Tell me about your work?"

"I had read the Bible with your eyes and I saw it. It was like an open vision, as real as talking to you now.
I was taken back to the tabernacle in the days of Aaron and I heard them and saw them in action."

~ ~ ~ ~ ~ ~ ~ ~ ~ ~ ~ ~ ~ ~

"I am so exhausted; this was a grueling day."
"Which day isn't Ithamar? I sprinkled the blood of about 500 burnt sacrifices today, cleaned them up and burnt them on the altar."
"Not to count the fire wood, the meat offerings and all the other holy rituals."
"It does take determination and dedication brother. It takes a special grace to be a priest and I am happy we have it."

"It is really an honor to serve the people and to serve God in this way."

"It is also very important for us to represent the people. Without God, we are not a nation. Without us, how can the people serve God as He prescribed?"

"That is why I am able to do this brother. It is an honor to be selected to serve God in this way."

"Indeed, it is. We stand between the people and their carnal rebellious ways. We facilitate them serving the Lord.

"And the people, they revere us. Almost worship us."

"Some envy us though. They say we have it easy. That we get provision without work."

"Pity they do not understand..."

"Yes, this is work, arduous work but it is a labor of love."

"Zzzzzz"

"Ithamar...Ithamar"

"Zzzzz."

"I guess there is no better way to express it than giving in to the demand of the body for sleep."

I am so tired too myself. Wish I did not have to get up to trim the lamps. God's instruction is that the lamp must never go out. Yaaaawn! The oil of intercession must keep burn...zzzz."

~ ~ ~ ~ ~ ~ ~ ~ ~ ~ ~ ~ ~

"My son," his father said, looking at him with understanding and appreciation in his eyes. "How do you interpret this vision?"

"Father, it is very obvious. Ministry is hard and disciplined work. To represent Christ in these end times will require the same dedicated obligatory discipline as the Old Testament priests.

No one's potential offering can be overlooked or ignored. Every sinner's potential sacrifice of their heart should be greeted, assisted and conveyed to the altar. We can never allow the light of our intercession to go out. Fire must always be burning on the altar. The work of the kingdom must take precedence to casual day-to-day life. It must be every believer's duty that places us in an obligatory responsibility to our heavenly calling. Father..." John paused. "Could it be that God wants to clothe every believer with the mindset of work and an attitude towards the end-time harvest as the Aaronic priesthood had towards Israel? Did He not make us all kings and priests?"

"Father, are you ok?" the concern in John's voice was evident and urgent. His father had attempted to laugh out loud and the sheer effort caused a ripple of pain to grip his face. John stopped his reflection then to attend to him.

"I am," came the weak response.

"You have gone well ahead of me. I am always impressed by your diligence but it appears the Holy Spirit has been teaching you Himself. This subject is at the very heart of His mission on earth. Check with history and our world today; every successful kingdom citizen has work ethics that is very disciplined and sacrificial. This is something every believer needs as the times progressively become eviler and more demonic.

The end-time harvest requires urgency and the attitude of work. Jesus is coming soon."

John listened to his father intently. His voice was still weak but his face had a pleasant and very radiant look. His father unconsciously loosened his tight grip on life just a little. He was a step closer to letting go now. He still needed to take his son further to cement this lesson in him. No, he would not let go of life just yet. He would determine when it is finished, not the doctors.
"Five days huh!" he thought. But yes, he would allow his sun to sink just a little.

"Son," he said, "tell me what happened to the casual and the distracted in the Aaronic priesthood. Also, what lessons can you find from the life of Moses to support this mindset of work?"
He knew his son would take this challenge seriously and even more so that his father was dying. He would not only research the topic but he would spiritually dissect it.
He smiled painfully as he saw the determination in John's eyes. It was mixed with a glint of tears as he shared his father's physical suffering. He was silent for a minute as he thanked the Holy Spirit for opening up John's understanding on this poignant end time issue.
"If the world gets it, I will have done more for the kingdom in death than in life," he thought. It was a thought he cherished. It was worth the pain of hanging on; the physical pain he felt every moment from the cancer in his body.

Before John knew it, his father was fast asleep. This was a welcome relief for John as he knew his father had not rested all day even though he needed it. He quietly slipped out of the room. As he left, he began turning over in his head all accounts of Moses he could recollect from the Pentateuch.

CASUAL PRIESTS

Assiduous, urgent state of mind
The care the things of God requires
The eminence of human lives
The saving grace by God's design
Cannot be casual with grace
Your offering that men be saved
It may come at the dearest cost
Your soul and many others lost

There was no trace of the sun when John stepped outside into the dusk. He was not ready to retire just yet. He needed some time to go over this moment spent with his father in minute detail. He wanted to review every thought, every expression, every emotion and the energy of the brief time he spent with his father. This meant so much to his father that he wanted to ensure not a single moment was missed. This meant so much to his father that he wanted to ensure he cleaned the plate, so to speak, and digested everything.

John could recount the dialogue and recite it from memory, but he needed to capture the spirit of the conversation. He also wanted to ensure he did not miss any of the unspoken lessons his father wanted him to receive. He wanted the gravy of the spirit of the lesson his father wanted to impart. Most of all He wanted the application his father hoped would impact his ministry and its effectiveness. John knew... he knew, his father wanted to impact him to impact his world. He wanted to pass on this message to his world in honor of his father and the Holy Spirit who endorsed every minute and was propelling these final moments.

John sat on a large rock and looked up into the night. A few stars danced lazily in the night sky as billions more pushed forward to make their glittery appearance as the dance progressed with the night.

John picked up a stone that was within hand reach and cast it into the valley. His distracted mind heard the echo of the soft mushy sound it made in the bushes somewhere.

He was fully engaged with his assignment. The sound of the rock reverberated in his focused mind as the moments passed, becoming a soft musical refrain, giving a backdrop to the reflections of his thought.

As the moments passed another sound got louder and registered. It was the unmistakable sound of music drowning the orchestra of the insects of the night. He frowned as the faint sound of a party in the distance interrupted his thoughts.

"How can people take life so casually in such serious times as these? Why must life be all about entertainment and 'feeling good' for so many? Why must people dance their lives away in the hype of a moment?"

He was thinking of more than just parties but of sins in all forms and the bad decisions of the millions who live to please themselves.

His heart tore as it settled on the church and the many in church who are uncommitted. Then he thought about the committed but too comfortable. They are satisfied just to maintain their position in Christ without pursuing the lost or rescuing perishing souls of others. He could see the many who quotes the Bible without the love that propels men to do something about a dying world; a ripe harvest spoiling in the fields of souls; a harvest committed to rottenness, death, worms and fire.

"Who are the lukewarm Christians Jesus promised to spit out of His mouth?" he thought. "Will many of these not be included?"

He could think of the many Christians and ministers who were winning souls but as a basic routine; who are not doing all they can do to 'scrape the pot' as they say, to reach that extra one they could have reached if they took that extra time and diligence, or the extra millions they could have reached if they took the time to invest themselves and of themselves in others.

So many lack the basic appetite for work! They have a kingdom concept but they lack the kingdom mindset of work. They are distracted by comfort, pleasure, personal pursuits and entertainment.

"Work huh! Distractions! What was that assignment father gave me?"

He could hear the words echo in his head.

"Son, tell me what happened to the casual and the distracted in the Aaronic priesthood?"

His thought reentered the closet of his reflections. It was then that he walked in on them in a moment of history.

~ ~ ~ ~ ~ ~ ~ ~ ~ ~ ~ ~ ~ ~

"It was worth it; it was well worth it Abihu," Nadab said to His younger brother.

"Did you see the glory of the Lord coming on all the people?"

"That was exhilarating. Did you see the fire coming down and consuming the sacrifice?"

"I saw it alright. I did not know that God would do that? And the people, I will never get rid of the sight of them shouting and falling on their faces."

"I could see that again any day."

"Do you realize how much that magnified our office? They fear and respect us even more now. We can do anything we want."

"What do you mean that it was worth it Nadab?"

"The sacrifice. That was work as it always is. I sweated a little."

"Meet too. Being a priest is hard work. We are butchers, we are lifting weight, we are cleaning the meat and cutting to specifications."

"Yes, and we lay them out as specified also. Even when we are tired, we follow the guidebook of Uncle Moses."

"And we are dancers. We wave part of the offering before God."

"Well father sprinkles the blood which too is work, and we also have to hold the blood for him."

"And we are sanitizers, we dispose of the blood."

"Yes, and we are intercessors and exhorters we bless the people, even when we are tired."

"Do you realize brother, everything we do is intercession? The offering itself is intercession. Our proclamation too."

"Sigh! Intercession is work, real hard, dedicated, committed work."

Abihu wiped the sweat from his face as he said this.

"It is, but now we know it can be very entertaining and exhilarating also. I will never forget how the people shouted and fell on their faces as the glory of God came down. We have the power to bring the glory of God to the people."

"Sigh! That part I could do again, anytime."

There was a moment of silence as the brothers looked at each other. Then as if sharing the same mind they said simultaneously, "Why not. Let's do it."

Nadab was silent as something like a hand of fear gripped his heart.

He shrugged it off and shook hands with Abihu as he said, "We will certainly do it very soon, brother!"

Nadab winked at his brother and said, "All day work and no play make ministry a dull game."

"Ministry is work, but it will be much easier If we mix it with entertainment. So much more doable if you make the work entertaining, even if we lose our focus just a little."

"You know brother, Moses forgot to include this when he wrote the script for our service. He only wrote about the work."

The punishing sun looked down on the scorched remains of the two priests laying there in the temple. Aaron's heart pierced him as he looked mournfully with tear-filled eyes at his sons. They had offered strange fire to the Lord by sacrificing without the necessary protocols stipulated. The fire of the Lord came as they desired but it consumed them and not the offering. God rejected the offering.

Aaron's emotions were fluctuating between his duty as priest to the God whom he loved so dearly and these sons he raised to walk in his own footstep. He could not shake the guilt that they died in the office he served, the only occupation he taught them.

He could see their hesitance from time to time as they embraced the work of ministry. He could not escape the enthusiasm in their faces when they saw the glory of God come down in response to their service. He knew he had them forever then, fully dedicated and with wholesome hearts. Well...so he thought.

Now he looked at them and his heart sunk as the sun did in that moment. A large cloud floated over its glorious parade and remained there for a short while. He saw them being dragged out by their uncles, brothers of their mother, with by their tunics as Moses commanded.

He heard Moses tell him along with Eleazar and Ithamar, his remaining sons that the kingdom mindset of work made no provision for mourning for the dead above their duty to the living.

In fact, Moses was angry with them for not eating the sin offering in accordance with the service ritual for the people.

Moses adjusted to the heart of the moment when they explained the difficulty in offering sin offering for the people when their own sons had no one to offer for their sins. They had experienced the punishing edge of the sword they dutifully shielded the people from in daily service.

Moses conceded that they could take the day but, just that afternoon. The work of ministry would resume in its dedicated detail, but for Aaron and his remaining sons the following day it would become harder with less hands to serve but equally necessary and detailed.

Moses himself grieved for his nephews but he had long surrendered to the reality, "The work of ministry must proceed beyond personal pain or problems of the moment. Instead, personal pain should serve as a reminder of the urgency of the many lives at risk. There is no room for selfishness in the kingdom; it is all about selfless service. My nephews sought entertainment instead of purposeful work to present and represent the people to God for the salvation of their souls, or rather, the atonement of their sins."

~ ~ ~ ~ ~ ~ ~ ~ ~ ~ ~ ~ ~ ~

John concluded in the moment, "When we forsake our mandate by Christ to satisfy our lust or ignore our mandate to do this it is wrong.

When we forsake our mandate because of personal problems it is selfish, self-promoting and ignorance of the urgency of the times. It is also an ignorance of the unusual opportunity to express faith in the moment to get God to break through on our behalf. We seek the kingdom and He solves our problems.

We must save the entertainment for heaven," John muttered. "Right now, the night comes, rather it is upon us when no one will be able to work."

John looked up and whispered, "Father, breathe into the hearts of believers the urgency of the time; impregnate us all with the kingdom mindset of work."

He spent a few moments praying in the Spirit to absorb and seal this prayer.

A dog barked in the distance as John went into the room to check on his father for a final time that evening. His heart warmed to see his father fast asleep with a most peaceful smile on his face. John drove out on the main street to cover the short distance home. He was there in less than five minutes. He avoided the town so he would not encounter any of the drunken revelers or the odd couples committing lewd acts in the shadows. When he arrived, he sat in his car for a moment and gave thanks.

"The wickedness of these evil times," he thought. His mind immediately drifted off in time. It went back beyond the days of King David and settled on two priests and a young prophet.

REBELLIOUS PRIEST

He could see them.
In the midst of a battle hot,
With blood being spilled a very lot
They were placed at the very heart
Yet they were so relaxed
They were positioned to change the game
It would take discipline and restraint
They chose instead to please themselves
And leave the people exposed to hell

The wrath of God so very real
The war that they could not perceive
The loss of lives or victories
Is fought on spiritual battle fields
Wasting time or on your knees
You put yourself or kingdom first
Ardent pursuit or frivolity
You action lives and destinies

O hindsight will cut you no slack
But foresight you have plenty of
For daily life is just a veil
See beyond, and you'll come awake
To the spirit world where there's no time
Judgment wraps every act with blazing fire

I t was a poem he had memorized.
John paused to catch his breath for he could see them. His heart was palpitating, his face sweating; his spirit mourning for he could see them...

They were sons of the high priest and heirs of the legacy of Aaron. They were aptly positioned to carry on the dignified legacy of priesthood. Dignified, because they stood between God and the people, but yes, it involved dedication and work and dedicated work. It was arduous. They were intercessors for the people and intermediary between God and the people. They performed the necessary rituals to remove the wrath of God from the people. Dignified because it brought them as closer to God than many humans could get at that time. It is difficult to represent God in this manner without entering into the heart of God. God called them holy, separated unto Him; His inheritance.

John gasped as a thought entered his mind. It is difficult to have God relate to you in this manner without coming under intense scrutiny. Mmmm... from both heaven and hell.
Are we not the temple of the living God? Are we not holy? Are we not kings and priests, a royal priesthood? Do we not have the Holy Spirit living in us? Something they never had or could ever experience. Are we not under commission to get involved? Do we not have a helper to make our yokes easy, a Governor to oversee this work and a Comforter to console us?

He could see them. His heart moved and his vision became blurry with tears. At a time like this, he wished he could not see at all. But...his heart moved; he could see them.

They knew their duties as priests but they did not know the Lord; they knew the rituals but did not know relationship; they knew the influence and privileges as priests but they did not engage the principles; they represented the work but they did not know the Word so they became presumptuous.

He could hear them, "Give me that. That is the meat we want. How dare you boil it! We want it raw. We are tired of pre-cooked meat."

"But God commanded..."

"We are His representatives and we are not asking, we are commanding!"

"Sob, sob!" John wiped his eyes.

Their voices were loud. They were aggressive and they used their influence as priests to be authoritative. The people reasoned with them, pleaded with them to obey the Lord but to no avail. The Lord had commanded in the law of Moses that the meat should be boiled; that the priests should use the fleshhooks and whatever part comes up should be theirs. The wisdom of Israel was no match for these two. They selected their portion before the ritual was performed. They totally abhorred the ritual.

"The mindset of work is all about compliance with rules. You cannot run your own race and expect a prize. You cannot defy the rules and not be opposed.

"Pastor, I cannot wait to reach heaven and to hear Jesus say, 'Well Done!'"

His pastor looked at the excited young man with

mixed emotions. He was a lazy person who was never engaged in anything the church did, no matter how excited he seemed. It was hard to find an answer that reflected what this boy needed to hear and yet maintain the role of a shepherd. The pastor looked down at him with a soft smile and said gently but firmly, "Well, get started."

His answer, even with his attempt at gentleness still startled the young man. "What..." he started, "what do you mean?"

"You cannot be done unless you are doing," the pastor wisely responded. "And to be doing well you have to be diligent in doing. In my many years of ministry son, I have seen many believers. Some who get in the work and some who are absent in the work but present for the reward. There are some who will speak well and some who will do well. Jesus identified these two in the parable of the father and his two sons. One excitedly spoke about going to work in his field but did nothing, the other did not have much excitement but He gave his energy. Kingdom work is not always exciting, therefore it demands character and determination. Yes," he smiled, "there are some who will do anything to see the work of God forwarded. They come out and get the church ready for meetings; are present for missions, attend services so regular you miss them when, or if, they are absent and they stay up at night and pray. They are usually the same people every time the church needs hands. Why? Because they have an attitude of work. A mindset to respond to their kingdom responsibility son. They genuinely love the Lord above themselves and want to do everything to further His work. I have also seen some who will promise you but never show up, and some who will not promise at all. They would never sacrifice their own agenda, television time and everything they do to get involved in where the heart of the Lord is...people. People are dying, going to hell but the urgency is lost on them. The bad thing is, some of them expect the Lord to reward them for doing Him a favor and getting saved.

Which of the two groups my son do you think will hear, well done?"

"The first," the young man responded.

"Which of the two groups are you a part of?"

The young man looked at the wise pastor and then looked away. He needed time to look into himself.

"Father, I must go," he said quickly and was off before he could get a response.

It was a conversation that he wanted to end but he knew he needed to finish, but not here. He was challenged to change. His entire attitude was under scrutiny; his very salvation; his attitude to Christ, to His work and to people. He had to finish this conversation by introspection in prayer. Today he would flex his muscles far above the fifteen minutes he had become comfortable praying for daily. As he went his heart struggled with the sacrifice, he knew it would take.

He was that young man. That was twenty years ago.

~ ~ ~ ~ ~ ~ ~ ~ ~ ~ ~ ~ ~

John could see them, these two priests. They were kicking at the sacrifice. They were pleasing themselves above the mandate of God and their duty to represent Him to the people.

"That is it!" he thought. "Pleasing their own selves huh!

It is impossible not to engage the Kingdom discipline of work if we put God above self.

This self-seeking, self-pleasing spirit is one reason the work of God is not furthered in the earth. Many believers are just like Hophni and Phinehas. Yes, that was their names, Hophni and Phinehas, sons of Eli."

He could see them, sexually assaulting the women who came to the tabernacle to seek God. This diabolical spirit moving them was self-serving and placed itself before God. Instead of building the people to serve God they diverted the women to please their own flesh.

"The kingdom mindset of work is kingdom-focused and not self-focused. It is intentional in fulfilling the kingdom mandate. It is about a battle. It is about being that good soldier who refuses to entangle himself with the affairs of this life."

A sharp dagger pierced John's soul as he saw them. They were many. Young men and young women from every continent whose sole intent for going to church is members of the opposite sex. He could see them, counselors, leaders, young people and other members who steal souls from the cross for personal encounters. They win the innocent away from Christ for themselves with no intent of lasting relationship.

He could see them plucking the spoils out of the bleeding side of the Lord Jesus.

He could understand the disgust the Lord must have felt with these two priests. They had no heart for the work of the ministry, or desire to further the cause of the Lord in Israel. Instead, just as the devil did in heaven, they openly competed with the Lord for these precious souls who came seeking Him.

John sighed. "It is impossible to have a kingdom mindset unless your mind is set on the King, His will and instructions for you. Until you are completely lost in love with Him and totally loving being lost in this manner. Until you love your neighbor as you love yourself. You can never steal from them to satisfy yourself. You can never steal the kingdom from them for whatever good excuse you may have. You love them to life and not to death.

Once you have a vision of Christ, it takes work, dedication, determination and a recipe of discipline and restraint to destroy all distractions and to make that vision a reality."

This thought stuck with him. He knew he would have to reengage it later, but for now he could not escape it.

"Father," he said that afternoon as he summarized. "The more I think on this, the more I am convinced. Is it even possible to be effective in life without a mindset of restraint and sacrifice?

Can anyone truly make it in any significant measure without sexual restraint, sleep restraint, and restraint in other areas of preferences including food?"

His father smiled. He knew it was impossible to look at the priesthood without embracing the discipline we all have to apply in every area of life to be effective in our assignment on earth. These have both physical and spiritual implications. There were also some physical things like exercise and health that complement effectiveness at work. The mindset is as much being as doing. You must be a worker with kingdom effectiveness at heart to do the work and maximize your time on earth.

He knew it was impossible to be completely fulfilled in this life without focus. Distraction will cause God to turn against you to destroy you and your works instead of turning His face toward you to establish and further your works.

Work without sound spiritual discipline is Babel, utter confusion. It makes your work a target for angelic defeat and a candidate for self-destruction.

This however was moving ahead of himself. He would get there but not yet.

"Son," he responded. "This is an assignment all by itself. The Lord has given you, my heart. I am resting so peacefully at night. Death is getting a beating by this vigor you are giving to me son. I look forward to hearing your revelations on Moses."

He fell asleep with a broad smile on his face.

MOSES

WORK YOUR WAY TO EFFECTIVENESS

He grew up in the palace as a prince with all the luxury, rights and privileges. He had the entire kingdom at his feet and the authority of being royal in the most powerful nation on earth then as a distinction. He was in no way ordinary, though he had a secret very few knew and no one really cared about: he was born a slave. Even if everyone knew it, no one could take his distinction from him. They would still have to bow to him; to jump at his command; to run at his orders; to dance to his beat. No one... well, but himself.

"It is like being born again into the kingdom of God, a son of God," John thought "No one can take that away from you, irrespective of what your history says; how poor, misunderstood, hated, sinful, or wicked you were. You have to surrender this royal positioning yourself. But then who would surrender a higher positioning for a lower; the kingdom of God for the devil's kingdom and world. Their wealth and authority in Christ of the kingdom of the earth, an old genie lamp, so to speak, for a new, beautiful, useless lamb... well, unless they do not understand what they have."
John thought about Eve; she was deceived. He

thought about the many who have left the church. They certainly could not understand. "Only by deception!"

His reflections returned to Moses:
He had the education and training of an Egyptian prince, the very best. He was a great warrior. Conquest built and sustained kingdoms then. It established sovereignty and dynasties. Kings would lead from the front in battles. He was prepared to be the best of the best. To defend not just himself but to defend a kingdom. To lead from the front. Little did he himself know that he was selected, chosen, educated and being prepared for his assignment from God. He would use all the skills learned to include palace protocols and palace association. It was an assignment he was not yet familiar with but he felt drawn to. It was an assignment he felt was linked to his root as a slave. The fact that he was a Hebrew was etched in his mind. His assignment was on behalf of the Hebrews; he knew that well. In fact, he felt that perhaps it was with the Hebrews. But then... they were slaves. So much to surrender. Either way, it would be very dangerous... unless of course he was Pharaoh. He could not escape the immediacy he felt. So drawn was he to his assignment that he ignored the protocols of his comfortable palace life and physically intervened in a dispute. It was a dispute between an Egyptian soldier who was accountable to him and the slaves who were answerable to him. He could easily have ordered the soldier to withdraw but no one was looking and he was angry. He killed him. He saw this as

an abuse; but what do you expect, they are slaves. No. It was an abuse of his people. He was angry. His intervention came as an expression of his anger.

He knew this could cost him dearly and it did. It was a clear display of unfaithfulness to his household, his kingdom and ultimately, his king. He chose to trust the person who he delivered. It was unspoken but a general expectation. He could not afford the news of what he did to escape to even this man's family. Rumor does not need communication cables to fly. Something told him his expectation of secrecy was unjustified, but in that moment, he did not care. He had made a decision. A decision Paul would speak about later in his epistles. It felt very good to him. The adrenaline pumped in his body like never before. He felt so connected to his purpose.

The very next day he went back to watch over a people he was passionate for. He intervened in an argument between two Hebrews and then, it hit home like a sledgehammer. Like a bath of icy water. He was unwelcomed and unappreciated here. In fact, they spoke to him, an Egyptian prince, as if he was lower than the ordinary soldiers. They offered him no acknowledgment, no protection, and no confidentiality. They would not dare speak to a soldier in that manner. They had something on him. Something that would cause him to lose everything and run for his life. He had no recourse to the palace. He was like a fish out of water grasping for breath.

He felt the hot desert sun on his face and the sand on his parched lips as he kept running. Running from a life he could not go back to. Running to a life not prepared for him. He had no idea what to expect, no relative to go to, no experience to help him. Running for life, or rather from life, just running... in the desert, not a place conducive to running; yet he had to run, just run. **The poet would later capture this:**

He was an Egyptian prince
Next to the king
But his heart was with the burdened and afflicted
Who were subject to him
Just ordinary slaves
O what a way
For a prince to surrender his exalted place

He reached out to them
To fulfill his heart
They dishonored him
And pushed him off
Made him the subject of Pharaoh's wrath

An Egyptian prince without a home
Friends, family or a place to go
No resting place under the sun
But an urgent cry
Run, Moses run!

In the words of Paul this Egyptian prince opted to suffer affliction with the people of God than to enjoy the pleasures of sin for a season. In other words, he preferred to join the toil of the Lord than to rest in the comfort he was privileged with.

He was spot on in relation to his assignment but spot wrong to think he could do it from his place of comfort in the palace.

Many Christians are willing to engage their assignment but not ready to sacrifice for it. They want to do it from a place of worth, but are unwilling to do it from a place of work and extreme sacrifice. They understand the call of the Spirit and the commission of their owner (Lord) and Master to go. **They have the loudest voices in church with their faces dripping powder instead of sweat.**

This Egyptian prince understood the principles of work and the techniques of battle, but he had never been to battle. He was to be thrown into live action on the battlefield of the wilderness. He knew how to put others to work without doing much himself, but now he was in a survival battle.

It was a battlefield that would sap his physical strength, test his mental capacity and drill him in ways he had never experienced or encountered before. It was an experience that would give him the Kingdom Mindset of Work.

It is impossible to be effective with our assignment on earth without clothing ourselves with the kingdom mindset of work. This type of work is, 'blood, sweat, tears;' 'whatever it takes;

until death no depart,' work.

Moses was being prepared to take a people through a similar hazardous journey he himself had experienced. It is impractical to take a people where you yourself have never been or to lead them to experiences you yourself have not been through. For those who attempt this, they become fragile leaders when they are tested with the test of the people, surprised by their surprises, distracted by their distractions and they lose hope with the faithlessness of the rest. It easily invalidates many leaders. Moses was being prepared to mentally deal with the hazard of a people he was naive in taking for granted before. He threw them a lifeline; they threw him on a sword. They were why he was running in the first place. They would keep him running every day that he would lead them. He needed the mindset of pursuance, resilience and perseverance. He needed patience to walk in the hazard of the wilderness and humility also to walk the wilderness in the hazard of the people.

For Moses, it turned out well. He came through and found accommodation and a wife. He got a normal job as a shepherd. On second thought, that was not normal; it required work where before he had worth. He had to stay out in the sun and in the dew at times. He experienced sleepless nights from time to time. He had responsibility for watching over dumb animals that would do dumb things all the time. He found character in correcting them with loving-kindness and gentleness. He found gentleness and humility in attending them, defending them, ensuring they were fed with the best word...I mean grass from the best pastures. It committed him to walking with them for long distances, taking them to the water and back.

He understood how to selflessly nurture them at all costs. He had to seek good locations and take them there and return them to the fold without losing any. He had a job.

No this was no ordinary job. It prepared him with the mindset, both physical and mental to lead a people on these same slopes and dry expanse of the wilderness. It came with the physical preparation of sweating for them and sweating with them. It positioned him to see the invisible hand when there was no water or food for his flock. It prepared him with patience for them and their many transgressions as he leads them into God's will. When they insulted him he did not take things personal. He knew it was the nature of sheep to do dumb things. It clothed him with the commitment to the fulfillment of his assignment above all distraction and beyond all diversions and drama.

The kingdom mindset of work eliminates all excuses on its path of fulfillment.

MOSES

WORK; OVERWORK; WISDOM WORK

Work is love's hidden command
Whatever kingdom life demands
Willing to do whatever it takes
Refuse the ridden flesh's dictates
The answer to the cross of Christ
Defend; avenge the sacrifice
To eye the promise, Beulah land
To bring its rest to fallen man

But work in rest may save the strength
Wisdom takes you to higher realms
To recognize the help you have
And utilize the willing hands
The heart engaged, the heart you pour
The more deployed; you attain more
For though the work is not reduced
Satisfaction rise on helpers used

Work wiser, work smarter
Work wider than yourself
Less effort, more impact
When you work with ready help

"My son, you cannot do this. It is not right. You will weary yourself and you are frustrating people. It is impossible for you to take on so much work and not get so burnt out that you become useless to the people and to your assignment. Yes, the work must get done. No, I am not suggesting that any be forsaken, that any soul be lost. I am saying that work is necessary but it does not have to be personal.

The nations must be reached but you cannot go to everyone yourself. Within your scope of influence and the resources available to you, mobilize and empower others to be an extension of your hands and feet. You focus on the harder cases, on coordinating your team and on senior management decisions. Select judges from among your leaders to judge the small matters. You deal only with the matters that require consultation with God."

When Moses' father-in-law left that day, his life had become so much easier. The work of dealing with the issues of the people, the kingdom assignment of discipleship had become so much easier. He was now engaging a system and not shouldering all the burden. Moses was able to take good advice but he was willing to take on all the work of ministering to the people even if:

1. He had to do it alone. **Are you clothed with this mindset?**
2. It sapped every strength and energy from him. <u>Are you ready for kingdom effectiveness in these end times? Are</u>

<u>you ready to work?</u>

3. It gave him little sleep and occupied all his waking hours. <u>Do you put sleep above reach and effectiveness? Solomon has strong advice for those who love sleep. They will be poor, physically and spiritually.</u>

4. It gave him no time for personal recreation. **<u>How much time do you spend entertaining yourself? How does your recreation time compare to the time you spend on His creation (engaging your kingdom assignment), your Lord and your commission to His beloved creation?</u>**

5. It wore him out totally, even to death. <u>How committed are you to the work of your kingdom assignment here on earth?</u>

Delivering a people from hell in these end times is a much greater mission than that of Moses. You will never find the heart of your mission unless you have a heart for the work that makes the mission possible.

POSITIONING FOR WAR

BATTLE ON YOUR KNEES

The sweat, the blood; the energy
The fire of the midday heat
The pain; the sacrifice compelled
The fight until the battle ends
Combat for life with no excuse
Wounds that offers no recuse
Attack may be your best defense
Watch! On this your weary life depends

Compels you to complete resolve
Resolves you to completely all
You've got to fight; you've got to run
No time for rest; the rest will come
Not in the battle; not in the flesh
The enemy seek your living breath
Monitors you with hidden eyes
Attacks your weak or prayerless nights

For just like this the war is real
Near misses gives you energy
So, with the good fight, you've got to be
Like lapping dogs on the battlefield

John could hear him as clear as the bird chirping in the tree. It was the expression of his thoughts not verbalized.

"They are trained; they have the skills, but I cannot let them do it all alone. I am too old to fight with them but I will take my place in the battle."

What would be the place for aging Moses in this battle?

"I will do more for them with my hand lifted in the air to God than I can do on the battlefield. I will intercede for them while they fight. No, it is not just enough to pray and leave it there. I will labor with them in prayer throughout this battle until I see them raise the banner of victory. God gave me the great commission to go. I cannot just sit here and expect the Joshuas of my day to do the work and hope for success. I cannot buy into success I have not participated in. The kingdom must advance; the enemy is real. I refuse to go to sleep and wake up to listen to the news of the battle. I refuse to sit in some quiet place secretly hoping, or to go about business as usual when the battle is raging so hot. I will clothe myself with the mindset of work and pray constantly and incessantly until I see them win. I will fast, with my hands lifted up before God and go through the physical discomfort of the battle until they pull through. I refuse to relent."

"Ah, these bones are old," he thought, as he pulled himself up to the top of the mountain from which point, he could see the battle. He was still very strong physically but he was well over one hundred years old.

He lifted his hands in the air and held them there. In his hands was his staff. Moses was standing sacrificially for Israel in battle. He could see them; Israel was on top; they were winning. He was intent to fight with Israel until they won. His heart was with Israel in battle but it was not good enough to have his heart full of Israel, he was determined to give Israel his full heart; to pour it out before God.

Time passed and his hands became tired, the muscles were straining. He questioned his commitment because of the sacrifice required. The question of Isaac to Abraham came to mind and he knew, you are not really sacrificing or working until your sacrifice question's you and say, "I see the fire and the wood, but where is the sacrifice?" Until the sacrifice becomes truly painful and incredulous. Until the sacrifice exhausts your physical capacity.

His muscles were asking the questions and he had no answer, his hands began to limp. At that moment he understood so clearly the significance of his sacrifice. He could see them, they could not see him, but the moment his hands fell limp, Israel began losing the battle. Yes, Moses understood, God gave the orders but the battle is as much spiritual as physical. It has to be taken in the spirit before it can manifest physically.

Israel could not see him; they did not know he was interceding. They could not see him sitting in the gates dictating the spiritual atmosphere of the battle. He knew every battle of life is dictated in the spirit before it is decided in the natural. No, intercessors may never be seen or even get the credit but their relevance and impact is very significant.

As his hands dropped a little, Israel began to lose. They were being pushed back by the Amalekites. The man of God shook himself in resolve. He could not surrender. As the hot sun fought against him, he lifted his hand to God. He could not allow his flesh to rule his spirit.

Immediately Israel regained the ascendency, they were winning again. But it was strenuous work. His muscles were unable to bear it. Those who lift their hands whether in worship or just lifting them for any other reason knows how a few minutes feels like. Imagine holding your hands up for thirty minutes with something, a rod, in your hand. Imagine how doing it for hours feels like. Imagine doing this outdoors in the day, throughout the day. This is the mindset of work that is necessary to advance the kingdom in these end times, just as at all other times.

Many of those who seems to understand the urgency of the spiritual battle are unable to orate it, they never seem to understand the work ethics needed. Few are willing to apply themselves to it. They know people are dying and they have the power to intervene but they are not mentally prepared to do so because of the sacrifice of personal comfort required. Not so for Moses, he was to stay in intercession until victory was secured. Prayer is not powerful until you feel that release in your spirit. You keep praying for as long as it takes until you get your answers. This is what Jesus equates to faith in Luke 18.

Moses had the heart, mind and spirit of intercession but he had moved beyond physical capacity, his hands drooped. He had reached his limit. He had the mind but not the power to keep going. Israel began to lose.

Should he resign himself to the thought that he was unable to make a difference? Should he give up in prayer? He had been standing all the time and his legs were hurting. He would not concur with the laziness that keeps others from praying unless they are lying on the beds under covers. Most Christians fall asleep laying in beds after three minutes. Moses would stand and pray. There was no sleep on the feet.

It was at that moment that he felt a hand on his shoulder. He looked around tentatively, afraid to take his eyes off the battle. His brother Aaron, the priest, had noticed what was happening. They understood, as many today, the importance of resolute battle on the knees until victory is complete. They saw clearly in live action that when the hand of Moses went down, when intercession slackened, the battle shifted. Israel was losing. They saw in living pictures the spiritual reality of end times intercession. When intercession pauses, Christians are hopeless in battle against the enemy. They understood that many Christians, families and individuals lose battles because they pray short prayers but refuse to be workmanlike and resolute in prayer until the battle is won. They refuse to be like the widow against the unjust judge in Luke 18.

Hur was there with Aaron. He was standing on the other side of Moses. They asked Moses to take a seat while they stood. They knew the importance of two or three touching things concerning the kingdom. They knew the power of agreement in intercession. Aaron and Hur held Moses' hands. They would keep the intercession going until victory. Someone needed to stand and they were prepared. They shared the burden of this intense spiritual warfare that Moses had initiated. Together they would win. They would not be overpowered. There is strength and power when intercessors stand together that individuals cannot generate alone, even when they are familiar with the presence of God, like Moses. Whenever they got tired Moses had enough strength in his rested hands to continue. This would give them rest and allow them to slacken a little until they held firm again for another session. They could see the battle and it encouraged them. They were winning. There was no slacking now. Amalek was wasting away. All their witchcraft and satanic backing had lost significance in the face of workmanlike warfare.

"That is it! The victory flag! We won!" Aaron celebrated. Moses, Aaron and Hur finally let their hands down and hugged each other. They ignored the sweat dripping down their faces and the soaked clothes they all wore. This was sweet, simply sweet. The teamwork was memorable. It made victory taste even sweeter. They worked for it; they worked through it together. They won with all Israel. Israel had won.

Joshua and all the warriors had a great report of victory to come back and tell. They themselves knew that winning the battle is not cheap. It is hard work. It is putting life on the line. The lives of an entire army. For one army to win the other must be defeated, decimated, and destroyed. The enemy would come with the intent of killing them all. That was the only way for them to win. Battle commits you to the kind of commitment that makes you forget the demands of your flesh. The cry of hunger, the pulls of rest, the punishment of the sun, the blessing of comfort and the sting and impediments of your wounds are all lost in the battle. It is all about your life. You are all in. The curse of passing time has no impact; you stay committed until the battle is over; for hours or for days. Israel would be rewarded with the plunder. The intent of the enemy is single: to steal, kill and destroy. In a kingdom battle, there is no giving up or turning back to run, it could mean death; yours and many others.

John reflected: a battle is pressing to victory, but when the instruction is from the Lord it is pressing from victory. It is still pressing, hard pressing, can even be depressing, although victory has been given, guaranteed, in the command to 'Go'. Kingdom effectiveness means arming oneself with the mindset of work. Victory is not there for the taking; it is yours for the losing. The kingdom is a battle and the mindset must be workmanlike.

Israel did it. They did not know then that the knee-work can be, must be, as intense as the field-work. They were never fighting alone; they would not be left to fight alone.

While they faced the physical reality of life and death there was another battle raging with equal spiritual resilience to engineer their win.

Whatever happens in the natural has a reference in the spiritual. This battle offers a firsthand glimpse into the spiritual world of intercession.

As John reflected, it became so clear to him then, "There is a call to intercession in these end times. It is a call to people who will sacrifice themselves in prayer. Who will wait in fasting day and night until they see the Lord Christ manifest. Who will resist sleep and pray in the spirit for hours or days; walking around on the feet until the legs get tired. Far beyond the nominal resistance of, 'Should I pray or not? Should I stand up or lie down? Should I do thirty minutes or one hour? A place where three hours become the minimum and only the Spirit dictates the end. There are some who have gone over thirty hours in continuous prayer. We are always winning when we remain in intercession. The devil knows he wins when the strength of Christians wanes in prayer. Those who are willing to pray until their hands get tired, until their knees get weak, until their clothes are dripping with sweat, will win.

The kingdom needs people who will prophesy and make declarations until their mouths are dry yet keep going. Satan directly targets the prayer life of believers. Our failing in prayer is necessary for his prevailing and end time manifestation of victory. The Amalekites (demonic forces) only win when your hands are down. Satan is ushering in the demonic age. Believers everywhere must pray, with all prayers and intercession with supplication in the Spirit."

John summarized his conclusion in his head as he went to report to his father, "The devil knows his time is short. He is raging and will even rage more as the time gets shorter. Jesus in the gospel, and John in the book of Revelations have sounded many warnings. The battle may seem rough for many but it is only just beginning. If there ever was a time for people with workmanlike intercession who understand that war never ends and we never sound retreat until victory; people who understand the spiritual consequence of not praying, praying less, or being prayerless, it is in these days. The devil takes no prisoners, he kills and destroys. As the days shift the mindset must shift that this spiritual battle is a real war and war is real effort: sacrifice, blood, sweat and tears. We must appreciate that warfare may result in physical damage, wounds and loss of lives, but we must fight to win.

John walked briskly to his father's room. He had a lot to say. "Father will be well pleased." He thought.

As John related his revelations on Moses and his attitude towards work, his father literally sat up in bed. It was for a brief moment. This was something he had not done for a long time. It was as if his son's relation of spiritual warfare, filled his bones with energy and nullified the pain. He was so caught up in the moment. He soon realized he was sitting up and groaned in pain and lay back down.

John groaned.

His father smiled trying to hide the pain.

"Mmm. My son. Spiritual warfare, mmm. It is the same as physical warfare, mmm. It requires work, exertion and commitment just as physical warfare, mmm. Physical warfare is futile without spiritual warfare, mmm.

Did not Jesus say in Luke 18 that we ought to pray always and never to cease? That the heart of God is good, unlike the unjust judge, but even then, our victory comes through perseverance in prayer, mmm? Did not Paul say, the effectual fervent prayer of a righteous man avails much, mmm? Did he not say to pray without ceasing, mmm? Are we not commanded to hold fast to the confession of our faith without wavering? To keep confessing until we receive the blessings, mmm? Did not Daniel pray and fast and kept praying for twenty-one days even when nothing was happening? He had the mind that he would not give up because his God answers prayers. Mmm, if our God answers prayers, the problem is not with the answer, it is with demonic blockage; the war in the heavens, Mmm.

Is that not what the angel told Daniel when he came after 21 days? He said the answer was released the moment the prayer was made but demonic principalities in the heavens blocked the answer, Mmm. The reason many do not receive their answers is because they pray surface prayers without fervency and effectual resilience. Many times, they stop praying too early. We know the answers are released. We are assured of the heart of the Father. He answers prayers. Jesus made this point clear but we must keep fighting. Just as with this example. Israel was fighting the Amalekites and there were demonic forces fighting with the Amalekites against Israel that were repressed by Moses' persistent intercession. Sometimes flesh causes us to relent and give demons power to steal our triumph.

We must approach prayer and intercession like obligatory work. mmm.

You know son, if I had the energy, ow!" He grimaced at his continuous painful effort to speak. John reached for him but he shook his head.

"My son, if I had the energy, I would set up twenty-four-hour prayer and intercession continuously in all of our churches.

It would be fed from the mission's department with a budget to include a stipend to staff but would be fueled by the involvement and participation of the entire church. It would be a platform for corporate, personal and overall international church victory."

John listened and nodded his head. His father had planted a seed in him. As he pondered this, he thought of the International House of Prayer. He was thinking beyond this expression of his father. He was looking at ways to get the entire church involved in workmanlike prayer from the churches both in the building, and believers at home. He was contemplating ways they could be hooked in together and participate even from home or work. "Father, give me wisdom to do this," he silently uttered.

"John, I am tired but happy. You have translated your daddy to heaven while he is still here on earth. I am the happiest person alive. You have nullified my pain. Your next assignment is to tell me about Moses' workman like attitude towards the word. Tell me of Joshua's and David's word and work attitude also. Give me their stories plus the stories of three to five others from the Old Testament towards work. Look at the entire books. Everyone whose name was mentioned in any significant way succeeded because of their kingdom mindset of work..."

His father fell asleep almost immediately after saying this. John was concerned because he had been laboring to talk. He went close and saw he was breathing steadily. His face was peaceful with a hint of a smile.

John was heartened as he left the room.

THE KINDGOM MINDSET OF WORD

WORKING THE WORD

The word your greatest source of strength
Your power and your best defense
It is the precedent of law
That spirits have no answer for
In this fiery spiritual fight
Where the battle is the war of life
It is credulous and so absurd
To know Christ and not know the word

So engage the discipline it takes
To engage the ancient kingdom ways
Commit the word to memory
And walk the path of victory

John listened to the soothing sound of the water gently rushing to shore as he slowly paced the beach thinking about the assignment his father had given him. A full moon was out and its reflection on the water was enchanting. It was a perfect setting to forget all assignments and get lost in nature's magical beauty. This he would not do. It was 2:00am. He had taken a trip to this beach resort just for the night. It was a personal retreat to give him the opportunity to think in a different setting. It was a place he often resorted to when he desired peace.

His meditation took him to the temptation of Jesus.

~ ~ ~ ~ ~ ~ ~ ~ ~ ~ ~ ~ ~

John could see Him in the wilderness, weak and thread-thin from forty days of fasting. His skin hugged His bones as if providing them the last shelter they would see before death and decay exposed them forever.

Then he saw the devil. He was an opportunist. He came to Jesus at His weakest moment and assailed Him in His area of weakness.

"Make these stones bread if you are the Son of God."

John paused as He analyzed this temptation. "It was a double whopper," he thought. The main course was aimed at the lust of the flesh at a time when His flesh was beyond the capacity to lust, it had a dire need for food. The second one was aimed at His pride at a time when Jesus probably needed the assurance that He was indeed the Son of God. His flesh was at its lowest point and could easily have cast doubts on His divinity.

Jesus responded to the temptation, not as God, but as man. He did so in the most effective language available to man in dealing with the devil. He did so with the greatest weapon available to man in their most vulnerable moments of demonic attack, the weapon Paul called the sword of the Spirit, the word of God. He used the scriptures available to Him then. He quoted from Moses, "It is written, man shall not live by bread alone."

The devil realized He had lost in the most stunning way. Arrows went deep into His spiritual soul and He was limping but He had to test Jesus in the other two areas of temptation. He went on to tempt Him with the lust of the eyes, "All these I will give you if you bow down and worship me."

He was referring to the kingdoms of the earth which he unveiled before the eyes of the Lord then. Again, Jesus responded with the word. "You shall serve the Lord Your God and serve Him only."

The devil was not just limping them but completely reduced as he forced himself to the last temptation.

"Many times we have the devil so backed up and defeated when we use the word," John thought, "but we do not know it for he keeps pressing in with his final breath."

This time the devil came with a full temptation of pride. Jump down from the pinnacle of the temple for the same word You quoted says He will give His angels charge concerning You."

Jesus pierced Him at the centre of His soul with His response. It was again the word that referred to Him as Lord; it was the commandment of Moses. "You shall not tempt the Lord your God."

Not only is He Lord in the world of man but Lord of spirits, angels and demons. The devil left

Him, completely repelled by the word with such precise use.

~ ~ ~ ~ ~ ~ ~ ~ ~ ~ ~ ~

John stepped close to the shore and allowed the waves to run over his bare feet as his toes squished the sand. He continued his meditation. It is apparent that the word of God is very effective to repel the devil. The Bible did say to resist the devil and he will flee. It is amazing even Jesus did not exercise His authority or command angels against the devil; He simply used the word. Is it that the word is the most effective tool on a spiritual battlefield available to man? Paul calls it the sword of the Spirit. Indeed, when you subtract S from sword you get word. The sword is in fact the s-word. Is it that the word is the most ancient yet most modern of weaponry in spiritual battles, not needing upgrades like the constant upgrade of physical weaponry? But how did Jesus get the word He needed in the moment to be so decisive? It is apparent that Jesus did not just quote the entire Bible. He selected His weapon, the word, well for each fight.

"No," John thought. "We cannot just use any word for every battle. If the devil comes with sickness, then we use, 'by His stripes we were healed', if he comes with sexual temptation, 'my body is the temple of the living God, I host the Holy Spirit, the most important Person on earth.'

Jesus did not repel the devil by His presence, or should I say, the devil was not repelled by the presence of Jesus in His earthly form. He did not repel the devil by using His name, although His name is very powerful. He did not repel the devil by fasting.

It is amazing that the weapon Jesus used is the same weapon available to us all, the word of God. Did not the scriptures say, God honors His word above His name?

But how did Jesus get the word in that moment? And how did He get the appropriate word to respond to the devil for each temptation? Did He have a script written? Did someone, person or angel, give Him the script and answers in advance or in the moment? Obviously not, He must have memorized the scriptures and known it so much that He had a ready answer to anything that came His way from the realm of the spirit. Is not the word spirit and life?

Jesus must have had the word in Him so much that He could select the right word for the occasion and direct it at the temptation, even when it was coming from Satan in person.

But John knew, Jesus could not have known the word in His human form unless he memorized it. He must have read it, studied it and meditated on it and in it. He must have deliberately memorized it. John could see Jesus taking a workmanlike approach to ensure the word was engrained in Him. Was it not the culture of the Jews to know the Torah by heart as a child?

It was then that the thought hit John like a piercing arrow. A light cloud had covered the moon and a slight drizzle was falling. It was dancing on the waters but John took no notice.

Was not His eternity at stake when Jesus took on

human flesh? Was this not one of His greatest sacrifices? He knew in the flesh He would give the devil the full opportunity to dethrone Him. Can you imagine what would have happened if He sinned? He would not only have left eternity but eternity would have left Him. He would be just like all the other angels who sinned and fell from their places.

Jesus understood the power of the word to repel the devil and He ensured He knew it. He worked the word as if He was studying for an exam as we all do; as if He was preparing for promotion. He was ever ready.

Is it not true, for us all, that our eternity is at stake? In these last days, it is even more necessary for us to take a workmanlike approach to the word as demonic activities escalate.

The drizzle had gone as quickly as it came. The bright moon was shining down on the sea creating the most beautiful scenery. A fish jumped in the distance, wanting to be captured in the picturesque moment.

That is what daddy wanted me to research. He did say Moses and his approach to the word. Moses inspired this word culture in the Jews which came from Jesus in heaven and which He quickly embraced and adopted in the flesh.

MOSES

THE WORD VISION OF THE WORLD

How far to go, to get, to hold
The thing you know you need the most
To what extent the sacrifice
To fill yourself with liquid fire
Can it be lightly cast about
The thing that you can't do without?
The sweat, the pain; the flesh withdraw
To get the word into your heart
To know just like a ready pen
Our heart had been its sole intent

So write it, read it, and recite
Your waking thoughts your dreams at night
The meditation of your day
The friend to greet you at your gate
The topic of your table talk
Your conversation as you walk
Until its puts all devils off
From the hidden recesses of your heart

John could see him as he laboriously climbed the mountain. God had commanded him to come up. His duty was to receive the word directly from God. He was amazed at the effort that Moses took to go and to get the word. The sweat was pouring down his face when he arrived at his destination. He had not eaten. Days passed and he would not eat, in fact, Moses was in the mountain for forty days receiving the word.

John played with the thought of forty days for a moment. "Forty days! A total fast. No food, no drink."

He startled for he heard a voice. He knew he was alone on this early morning beach trek. He settled when he recognized the voice. It was the voice of Moses but it was only given life by his own meditation. He was stunned to silence as he eve-dropped on Moses' intimate conversation with himself.

"It has been thirty days; my body is being pushed to the extreme but I am in the presence of God. I am receiving His word and I am willing to sacrifice for it. It is as if my body does not need this food. The word has become to me the food that I need."

"Much more than my necessary food," John smiled. This thought was inspired by Job, but the spirit was Moses in the moment. It was Job's lifestyle.

It was after forty days that thin Moses carrying two tablets of stone came down the mountain. They were heavy but the value of the word that was written on them was weighty enough. As he gave the word to the people he was reminded of the first tablets he has received. These he broke because of the rebellion of a people. It sunk into his heart at that moment that the people of God are always in a spiritual battle. The only thing that separates the winners from the losers is the word of God.

"Isn't that what determined the victory of Jesus when he was tempted by the devil?" John smiled to himself and went back into his meditation.

He saw Moses giving the law to the people. Throughout his time God would give him many ordinances. In fact, he was credited to have written Genesis to Deuteronomy. All the experiences in Genesis pre-existed him but he received it by revelation as if he was present. Moses had responsibility for the word and for the people. He had to enforce the word to the people.

John could hear Moses say to himself, "I have to remind myself of these laws daily and throughout every day. At any time, someone may come to me for justice. I cannot speak from my own resources or my own mind, I have to judge their cases based on what the word of God says.

In fact, the word of God is the only law that exists here. I have to know it.

John could see the reality of learning the scriptures. They were not yet captured in the Bible. Moses poured himself into the scriptures. These are the same scriptures he himself had written. Moses did not read from a script when he dictated Deuteronomy to the people verbatim in his final days; he had it all in him. Hearing the scriptures is good but if the scriptures are going to be of any great use to anyone, he has to know them, to memorize them.

~ ~ ~ ~ ~ ~ ~ ~ ~ ~ ~ ~

The clanging of iron against iron filled the air as the small dusty streets got busy with soldiers preparing for war. There was the grinding of metal as swords were being sharpened while others were being made. Women stood in the doorway obviously anxious; some very fearful. They were unsure if their husbands or their sons would return from battle alive.

"Daddy that is the trumpet!" Ieze said.

His father, Esiac, rushed into the house.

"Why don't you join the others father?"

"I have to go pick up my sword son."

"But daddy…"

Ieze was just four years old and did not understand. His father had no time to explain although he really wanted to do so as at the other times before. He looked at Ieze and waved.

"Ieze would never understand," he chuckled as he thought about it. Can you imagine an army coming against Israel and we have no swords to fight with? Can you imagine the chaos if we had our metalsmiths on the battlefield making swords while we are fighting?

Wow! That is most hilarious. That would be a walkover. We and our metalsmiths would all be dead."

John paused as the conversation between Esiac and Ieze replayed in his mind. Isn't that what Christians do? Aren't we always on a spiritual battlefield? Isn't our enemy ever going about as a roaring lion seeking those who are unprepared that he may devour them? Does he ever relent? Does he ever sleep?

If there ever was a time that warriors needed preparation it is now. Warriors, why did I say warriors? Ordinary believers. Well, warriors. Isn't that what Paul tells us. He said, "Fight the good fight of faith."

We are always in a fight. "Did he not also exhort us that those who do warfare cannot entangle with the affairs of this world?"

John chuckled as he thought about his favorite scripture in Ephesians. A security guard waved at him in the distance and he waved back. The gentle splash of the sea was providing a harmonic natural backdrop for his thoughts. The night was slowly drifting. It was getting darker as the bright moon had a private moment behind a cloud.

Ephesians 6 it is. We do not fight against flesh and blood but we are in a fight. What Paul wanted to establish was that believers are constantly in a battle. It is even more severe and intense than physical battles. It involves unseen foes. Because we cannot see them does not mean they do not exist. The spiritual world is more alive, more active and much more powerful than the physical world. Accepting Jesus as Lord sets us against His demonic foes.

 The problem is that they cannot be seen, just as pandemic viruses, and that makes them multiple times more dangerous.

Paul wants us to accept the reality and the severity of our situation. To understand that spiritual battle needs spiritual weapons. The word is spirit and life. He charges us to be ready and fully armored all the time. We cannot afford to take off our armor. We cannot afford to leave the word or have the word leave us. Our sword is our weapon to attack the enemy but also to defend ourselves.

Isn't this what Jesus used to defend himself when Satan attacked Him in the wilderness. **Not only must we have our sword, sharpened and ready, we must be trained how to use it, and we must keep practicing so we are never dull. Training never stops. Our body must be synchronized with our weapon, the sword.**

John returned to the scene between Esiac and his son Ieze. And he saw as Esiac grabbed his sword and ran to join the army. He settled in his rank as they prepared themselves for battle. He could hear him say, "These times are very testing for Israel. We have battles so frequently now. We have to be ready all the time. I can remember the time Nehemiah had all the builders on the wall sleep with their sword at hand."

~ ~ ~ ~ ~ ~ ~ ~ ~ ~ ~ ~ ~ ~

"So how do you prepare in these end times?" John thought.
He could see them. He could see them everywhere. All Israel was doing it, both the young and old. They were constantly repeating the books of Moses as they walked, as they worked, as they talked, as they played, whatever they were doing.
"You shall love the Lord. You shall love the Lord with all your heart; with all your heart, yea, and with all your soul and with all your strength."

"Daddy why are you saying that so often?" one boy asked his father.

"My son, this is the Lord's command through Moses. I must memorize it and live it. I must remember them to perform them. I must keep it before me always. That is the command of the Lord our God through Moses. What did I just say my son?"

"That Moses commands it".

"No my son. What did the scripture say?"

"That I should love the Lord my God with all my heart, with all my soul and with all my strength."

"Awesome son!"

"Daddy, I know the scriptures too."

"It is very important, son. I am so happy that we have this culture that cultivates a mindset of the word. In fact, it is God who commanded us in Deuteronomy six that these words that Moses commanded us should always be in our hearts. You know son, the word will always be on script and available to us, but it cannot be in our hearts unless we place it there.

Moses did not just give us the instructions; he gave us the formula. He instructed us to teach them diligently to our children, to talk of them when we sit in our houses, to always repeat them when we walk by the way, when we lie down and when we rise up. In fact, the word of God has to be in our every conversation. How do I respond when somebody comes and asks me, 'Oh how are you today?'

Well, I say, "I feel a bubble of life. My strength is renewed like the eagles. I feel like a king surrounded by so many angels assigned as my

body-guards. I am so in love with God; His praise will never leave my mouth;"
I use the word my son.

John shifted his thoughts again to the instructions of Moses. "You shall bind the word as a sign on your hand my son, put them before your eyes always as frontlets. They must guide your vision. Write them on the doorposts of your houses and your gates."
Indeed, everyone who comes in must know that this house intends to walk in obedience to the word of God. They must know, the Word of God, Jesus, dwells here. Most importantly though, the word is clearly visible for recital and memorization. Interestingly, our spiritual gates as the temple of God are our hearts. When we enter these gates we must be reminded of the word of God. We have to write it in our hearts.

John could hear the conversation resume.
"Daddy, we do everything Moses commands us to do. You never allow us to vary. That is why I know the word so much."
 "My son, you are an Israelite; this is our heritage."
"Did you know daddy; this charge is not just in Deuteronomy 6 but it is repeated in chapter 11?"
"I know my son. It is repeated for emphasis. Why don't you tell me what it says?
"It is very similar dad. Lay all the words I have commanded you in your heart and in your soul. Bind them as a sign on your hand. Place them before your eyes as frontlets. Teach them to your children. Remember dad, you told me that Moses told you to teach them. Not just to repeat

them, but to explain them and to ensure that we also learn them.

You are to speak of them when you sit in your house. We must always talk about the word daddy. God commanded a culture that was embedded in the word. We must include it in our conversations when we are eating, when we are walking; when we lie down and when we rise up. "

John could hear himself saying, "Living the word is a mind-set; we are required to work the word until the word builds our world, or rather becomes our world. As it applied then it is even more poignant now. It is a kingdom mind-set that takes effort, discipline, sacrifice and work."

John saw the satisfaction in the father's face as the son continued, "You shall write them on the doorposts of your house, you said that, and on your gates. But then you told me the reason we do this is that our lives will be extended. Dad, you told me we do this so that the days of our children will be multiplied in the land. That this is the promise of God for those who are deliberate with the word: as long as the heavens last and the earth lasts, we will be rooted. It goes beyond this; it is an eternal promise."

~ ~ ~ ~ ~ ~ ~ ~ ~ ~ ~ ~ ~ ~

John felt the blanket of sleep descend upon him like a fog. He reluctantly said goodbye to the peaceful shores once again illuminated by the brilliant moon.

The kingdom mind-set of word is much

more than just studying or reading the word or listening to a sermon in these days. We have to go back to what Moses taught. We should be memorizing the scriptures and speaking the scriptures in our every-day conversation. Our day should be sculpted with scripture. The scripture should be a part of our daily discipline to prevent us from being attacked by the enemy. It is necessary to keep us grounded in this end time's wrath of the devil.

What is lacking is that we have the Word, Jesus, but we do not know the word; we have the Word but the word does not have us; we are so distracted.

We exercise faith but it is not mixed with the word. Our world is in chaos because there are many Christians who are fighting...God knows what, but they have not committed the word to their hearts.

What is this about being prosperous? If there is ever a time we need a formula for prosperity, it is in these end times. Pandemics, wars and natural disasters have taught us that prosperity is a myth unless it is based on a spiritual formula. Many wealthy organizations that have built their wealth on standard formula of debt financing have gone belly-up. Believers and non-believers alike have had seen their income eroded. The uncertainty at times has caused nervousness. Is there a word formula?

John remembered his father had asked him to research Joshua's approach to the word.

PROSPERITY FORMULA

DIVINE SECRET FROM GOD HIMSELF

The world you work, the world you try
Success may come or be denied
From God's own tongue, secrets revealed
The word your safest guarantee
Work the word it works your best
Extra-ordinary; yes, good success
Success that standards can't define
That baffles theories and science
And impacts time with eternity
And imprints time with your legacy

Ordinary men with stories told
That never ages or go old
Though the secret is not often taught
The word was living in the heart
Eternal word; the world of men
Sun stood still and giants fell
The words when living on the tongues
Make the ordinary a walking gun

Moses was dead. Joshua was befuddled. He had lost a mighty leader and great expectation was on him. Everyone knew that Moses had raised him to be his successor.

They heard Moses charge him with leadership. Joshua knew that his own training or strength was not adequate to lead this people. He was praying. He had spent the time praying. He was still holding on to his memory of Moses. He was still turning over in his heart the formula Moses used to lead Israel, trying to decide how best to proceed. It was then he felt that presence. That presence that caused him to fall on his face and remain transfixed. He heard the voice.

It was the voice of God and none other. He said, "Moses my servant is dead."
"There it goes," Joshua thought. "All the concept of trying to lead like Moses. God was not commissioning me to do this. I have to lay that to rest with Moses. God was giving me my own commission; my own mandate."
He heard God tell him to go over Jordan with the people. He had given him all the land he walked on. God charged him to be strong and of good courage. What stood out was when God reiterated to Moses, "Observe and do all the law Moses commanded you. Do not turn left or right from it and everywhere you go you will prosper." It was then he got the formula. The formula that made Moses so successful. The formula Moses taught the people. The formula that is relevant to every mandate, every person, in every dispensation and every age. It was the formula that sustained Moses and all Israel through the grueling years of the wilderness age and the formula that will sustain believers through the grueling years of the end times. It will be O so very relevant then, with all the viruses,

earthquakes, famines and persecution prophesied. It is a spiritual formula necessary to keep believers alive and successful in the end times when the devil and his demons become even more rampant.

The word of God speaks of the devil having great wrath for he knows his time is short. Can you imagine the wrath he will demonstrate as his time gets even shorter and he draws closer to his fiery end, or rather, fiery-eternity, or should we say, fiery non-end, or rather, non-ending fire?

Joshua heard the voice of God and registered every word and syllable. "The Book of the Law, the Word of God, must not depart from your mouth."

He did not say from your bedside table, or from your heart. He said from your mouth. The formula is only active if the word of God is spoken. It will require a workman-like attitude of dedication. It is just as Moses taught. Yet for it to be coming from the mouth it must be committed to the heart.

God was not finished, "You shall meditate in it day and night."

He did not say, read a verse. Spend five minutes, or an hour. Have a set time and when you are finished feel accomplished.

The formula requires us to soak ourselves in the word and make it the basis of our day. It should permeate our thoughts during our work day and other daily activity. Did not Moses say to speak it when we lie down and rise up, when we are walking and talking? What is God saying differently? Nothing!

"This will cause you to observe to perform everything in it. In doing this you are guaranteed prosperity in everything you do and you will have good success. Your success will not be ordinary."

Joshua heard the voice of God. It was a very plain formula for success. It was not a work-hard formula; it was a word-hard formula. It was not a work the world or work like the world formula, but a work the word formula. It is a spiritual mystery with a physical guarantee that most will miss because it is not the way of the world. He repeated the revelation handed to him directly from the mouth of God, "The Book of the Law, the Word of God, must not depart from your mouth."

Indeed, this was the formula for unusual success; extraordinary success; exceptional success, or, in the words of God Himself, good success."

People will later talk about the walls of Jericho falling flat, but they will not talk about Joshua's constant meditation in the word. They will not speak about his day-in day-out muttering of the word. They will not speak about him lining up all his conversations and responses with the word. They will speak about the sun standing still but they will not speak about his word-conditioning that cultured his faith and committed nature to a captive response to his voice.

In fact, Joshua did all the work in the word, meditating in it, speaking it, making it the basis of his life and breath. When it came to the actual battles, the word did all the work for him. It is a formula that always works: work the word and the word will work for you; live the word and the word will make you win. Joshua understood by crunching the word and registering successes that all his battles are spiritual and the word is the key to victories.

People will speak about Joshua fearlessly confronting a spiritual being, the commander of the army of the Lord, and asking him, "Are you for us or against us?"

They will not speak about what Joshua knew. He was filled with the word and anything that came against him comes against the word in him and is already defeated. In fact, when you are full of the word you become dead to the world and the word becomes alive in you; your life is hidden with the Word in God. Whatever comes against you, whether spirit, or flesh; angels, demons or men, has all reason to fear, not you. They may defeat the world but they cannot defeat the word. Meditating in the word in the manner God prescribed to build the kind of faith that some may call a supernatural gift.

What people often ignore is that faith comes by hearing the word. There is no greater inspiration for faith than hearing the word from your own mouth.

Joshua knew his formula was fool-proof. It came from the mouth of God itself. There is no greater authenticity of spiritual revelation. **The Kingdom mind-set of work, applied to the word is the greatest asset of believers in the end times.** Believers must have a positive word attitude and mentality to stay above the fray in trying times.

Success and survival will be dependent on their approach to the word. Some take a causal approach and expect good success. Others sweat the word and calmly approach life and whatever the devil brings with confidence and the guarantee of answered prayers every time. It is the driving force behind the end-times prophetic move as evidenced in Nigeria.

Success against temptation, persecution and every attack of the enemy is a word problem. Spiritual things must be resolved with spiritual tools. It however requires the same arduous dedication and pursuit. The word must be worked with dedicated deliberation.

The darkness was fading as the sun made its way behind the clouds. Morning was approaching. John's adrenaline was pumping with these revelations and he was not ready to go to sleep just yet. He turned his attention to David.

What did David say in Psalms one? Everyone who meditates in the law, the word of God, day and night is blessed. In fact, he shall be like a tree planted by the rivers of water. His leaves will never wither and anything he does prospers.

Isn't this very similar to the language of God? Meditate in the word of God day and night; all the time. This will guarantee good success. David broke it down even further. He said, "Whatever, anything; everything that person does will prosper; will be successful. Nothing that person does will ever fail.

No wonder David was called a man after God's

own heart. He understood the heart of God; he sought and discovered the heart of God and he worked it.

Goliath did not just fall on a sling stone; he fell on the word as did the lion and the bear before.

A lot is spoken of David's victories but little is told of his time in the word. A true picture of David is of a man spending every available time in the word and in meditation. As David puts it himself, "In His law, I meditate day and night."

"Well John, it may not be true to say little is told of David's word crunching habit. He told the story himself in all the Psalms he wrote. They all came out of his meditation and worship times. His devotional habit and lifestyle decorates the worship of so many today and throughout time. In Psalms 119, David paused, just to eulogize the word, to celebrate the word, to appreciate the word, to commit himself to the word, to declare his confidence in the word and to commit himself to a good word habit. It is the longest Psalms and the longest chapter in the Bible. If the word is the most important piece to our spiritual puzzle, it follows that we must spend the greater amount of our time on it, with it and in it," John said, correcting himself.

Walking in success is walking in the word. If ever there is a time that we need the kind of success that allows no margin of error, it is now, the end times. As the season of darkness becomes fiercer and more intense, we will be thrown into a world-puzzle that only word-preparedness will extricate us from.

We have to know the word in this time. It cannot

just be on occasions but as a necessity of life. We work a profession to become successful. Years are spent in university to become a doctor or a lawyer. The word is our spiritual university for every area of success, good success, success that extends throughout time and beyond; success that is time-tested yet timeless; it is recognized in eternity and rewarded with stars.

In this demonic age, witches and demons will fight believers from their high and elevated platforms on earth. Our main basis to fight back is the word. We have to fill ourselves with the word of God. Read the word, regurgitate the word, record the word and listen to it, meditate on it and memorize it. The CWDS Bible written by the author of this book is such a treasure, in these times. It presents a new and exciting way to read the word with notes, quotes and prayers. It is one of the many tools available to believers today to assist their word habit, but the onus is on them to make the word their world. Not just to fill themselves with sermons and commentaries but to fill themselves with the word.

~ ~ ~ ~ ~ ~ ~ ~ ~ ~ ~ ~ ~ ~

John quickly undressed, set his alarm for eight o'clock and sunk into the comfortable bed. He was very tired but he could only afford two hours sleep. He had so much to do today. He would have to find a balance and get some sleep later today. He would also eat well and exercise to ensure his health was not affected by his hectic work habit.

Four hours' sleep would normally be enough for

him, but he would also listen to his body and respond when it speaks. Today he had accomplished a lot and he was satisfied. He would never have surrendered these revelations to sleep. He could not imagine how much value people have lost and by extension the world, by sleeping too much. He reflected on a rhyme he learned in primary school:

The heights of great men, reached and kept (sustained)
Were not attained by sudden flight (overnight lottery-success)
But they while their companions slept (played around, partied, entertained themselves)
Were toiling upwards in the night.

John could feel his head sink into the soft pillow. It had the smell of a flower garden. "Nice fragrant fabric softener," he thought.

That is all he remembered until the angry alarm woke him two hours later. He was too tired for that level of argument but to maintain peace he got to and grudgingly went to the shower.

DAVID'S MINDSET

A JOB WELL DONE BUT NOT OVER

John sat at his desk at work just reminiscing on what he had previously done. More than ever, he understood the importance of an attitude of work and resilience, to achieve success in the kingdom. A thought took him back to King David.

He could see King David working his way to the finish line. He did not stop investing himself in kingdom business until he got there; literally until he died.

David was inactive on the battlefield. His men restricted him from going to war when he fainted on the battlefield due to his age. He was almost run over by a giant then. As a young man he was fire; as an old man he still carried that fire in his spirit. David was not one to sit still. He tried to stay home once and got in trouble, so much trouble, it cost him dearly. At that time, he could go to battle but remained and got distracted.

John paused and, in his mind, he could picture the many ministers of God getting distracted during the coronavirus pandemic. It is the first time the church has been forced into world-wide lockdown. The devil knows it is hard to take out a warrior/minister on the battlefield, with the battle mind-set, but it is something different to engage a minister with a battle mentality but who has been inactive. Unless that person finds spiritual preoccupation in an adjusted routine, he becomes a target. His skills are not as sharpened; his mind is not as alert in the word, and if they do not have a word study and meditation habit, they may be drained of the word.

David knew this well and he sought for everything he could do for God and for the kingdom in his old age. He ensured he mentored and trained his son Solomon well but he needed more. Not only did he need more but he refused to go to his grave full. He wanted to ensure that all that the Lord had deposited in him was released to the kingdom. He wanted to go to his grave empty.

~ ~ ~ ~ ~ ~ ~ ~ ~ ~ ~ ~ ~

John could see him. The King sat there reclining in his garden. It is a place he loved to resort to. He had the most beautiful flowers imaginable, well-tended. It was perfected with a few colorful exotic birds, cultured by expert hands and expert care. It is a place the king loved to resort to. He knew with human touch you could create anything of excellence. The thing he could not create was the golden sunset that played a most excellent tune on the already colorful and beautiful scenery. It is a moment that goes straight to his heart. It was a visual sound that gave perfection to music and made music to perfect the garden in a way that instruments or voice could never achieve.

It is a mystical beat that engages you and keeps you captivated; that relaxes you and releases the creativity in you. At that moment the mind of the king centered on his God. Whenever he had moments like this his thoughts would erupt with love for God. He would write music and psalms. His creativity would erupt and he would think of new musical instruments to capture the beat. This time he was thinking of doing something, another thing very significant for his God. He was thinking a thought he had entertained for some time now. He wanted to build a temple for his God. As the sun sank and the magic snapped his thought matured, "Yes, this is what I will do".

It was not long after, he called Nathan, his seer, his personal prophet and he replayed the thoughts to Nathan. Nathan came into agreement with him immediately. He knew that David was a man of God and the things that came into his heart always abounded to the pleasure of God. He felt that there could be nothing wrong in building a temple for the God they so loved and so he conceded. As he left God turned him back with a message for David that this task was not for him. His assignment was wars; the building of the temple was for his son Solomon.

David felt restrained, somewhat a little bit defeated. He wanted to work every single day of his life for God. He would fight His battles; write His songs; lead His people and worship Him and love Him. He would work for God every moment of his life; until his energy was fully sapped and his eyes closed in death. He wanted to be effective for his God and in service of his God. He was disappointed but he conceded to the wisdom of his God.

"At least" David said "If I cannot do it myself, at least I can give all my strength and my energy in preparing for my son Solomon. I can make it easy for him. I can spend the time in getting the resources and making the connection. I can lay aside gold and silver and make provision for this temple. At least I can organize and structure the people for the temple. At least I can prepare my son Solomon."

David smiled as memories took him back to when he was a little boy on the fields of Judah tending his sheep. There was never a moment in his life that he did not give his all. He could remember being wet by the dew and the rain on the open fields, being burnt in the sun in the days but he took care of the sheep.

"Nathan" he said as he sat talking to his seer.

"I was never comfortable losing a sheep. I went through everything the sheep went through, I tended them. I found the best pasture even if it was a long walk away. Sometimes I was sweating and totally exhausted and when the sheep were scattered I did not rest until I brought them all back, I counted everyone. I remember a lion coming against the sheep; how dare him! But I had the anointing of the Lord upon me. I lived in prayer and worship. I wrote songs and psalms but something happened when Samuel anointed me, I rose up with holy anger. Some would say I was dumb and perhaps I was. Why should I risk my life for sheep that we were going to kill anyway and eat? They were under my charge Nathan and I give everything for whatever I am responsible for. Consider me a man who swears to his own hurt but never changes, never shift. If I say I am going to do it, I lay my life on the line. I went after that lion. It roared at me, came with all its strength at me, but I smote it and killed it. Another time a bear came, big and powerful; strong and fast. You don't mess with a bear but I tell you, tell the bear or whatever they are, not to mess with my sheep. I slew that one also. I took care of my sheep. I thought about them".

"My king," Nathan said, "that is why God gave you responsibility for all Israel, he knew you would take care of them just as your sheep. He knew you would defend them, fight for them, give your heart for them, lose your sleep to ensure they were safe and covered."

"That is my heart Nathan, that is why I feel so strongly about this temple. Israel needs the presence of God, the house of God with them constantly."

"God will give you your heart David but this is not your responsibility, it is Solomon's."

"I know; I have accepted that my prophet."

"I remember when Goliath came against Israel, everyone was fearful and running away. A holy anger came inside of me. I said, who is this uncircumcised Philistine to defy the armies of the living God? Nathan, I understand spiritual things. What we see today is not a lion or a bear, or Goliath but a manifestation of the devil raging. Constantly raging at the people of God."

"David my king, I wish that every person in the kingdom had your spirit. The spirit of a warrior; the spirit of work. Then we would never be defeated; we would always advance. My King, when you took charge you were surrounded by enemies all around: by the Philistines who constantly fought you, you went against them, never once were you defeated. You brought down many angry and mighty enemies of the people of God. You depended on the hand of God, the leading of God. You would never go up arrogantly but you went and you sought God for each battle; even as you asked counsel in building the temple. I remember when God told you to wait until you hear the sound of movements in the mulberry tree. He said He would have gone up ahead of you and strike the Philistines. You depended on the counsel of God and defeated all your enemies. You fought a good fight my king; you never backed away from a battle."

John paused as this conversation played over in his mind. He could see the demons, the witches, the anti-Christ, all the enemies of the living God raging against the people of God in the end times. He knew that the heart of David, the mind-set of work, is what the people of God needed. He could see kingdom citizen depending on the living God, leaning on the living God, ready to advance the kingdom in the face of raging enemies. This is the spirit that must be recaptured and regained in these times for the kingdom to move forward. Now he understood why his father wanted him to reflect on these things.

John paused and listened and reflected on that moment. He could see Nathan still speaking to David, he said to David, "My king you are extraordinary, you are always leading the people into battle."

"That is what kings do" David said.

"You were at the forefront; you fought like any ordinary warrior. You are not like some to stay behind and watch it happen as you preserve yourself, you were at the forefront. You did not sit to enjoy the comfort of your palace while your warriors went out to work. You went ahead of them."

Kingdom citizens, John thought. We are kings and priests but how many of us have the mind-set to work? We sit and we try to enjoy the benefits of our connection with God and the benefits of the kingdom. We want to live comfortably and to live in pleasure, but Jesus himself said seek first the kingdom and all its righteousness and all these things will be added. It requires the mind-set to work. Now I understand.

He went back to the conversation.

"I remember," David corrected Nathan.

I remember the day that I sent the army out to battle and I stayed home to enjoy the comfort of the palace. I woke up and I saw Bathsheba bathing and I took her, I committed adultery, I committed murder, I sinned. I remember you came in and corrected me and how I repented.

How I was caught up by my own action, but God was gracious to me."

"David my king, that is what happens when kingdom citizen does not have the mind-set to work. When they take a day off, then the devil takes every opportunity to attack them, to deceive them. Every time you see a kingdom citizen that is not actively engaged in war, that is not advancing the kingdom of God, they are deceived. We are constantly at war and there is no neutral ground. We must clothe ourselves with the mind-set of war and war is exertion and assertion. We can't be on the defensive all the time, one day our defenses will be breached. We will be caught with our guard down. We must also be on the offensive. It requires a different type of energy with the mind active and alive. We have to be ready to vanquish the enemy and create the conditions of peace. It is the condition you have created from which Solomon will benefit in building that temple of God. One day my king, the earth will need kingdom-minded citizens who will create the conditions of peace for an earth in deception to the devil, for a world that is spiraling towards destruction. The conditions of peace may not happen in our lifetime or in their lifetime but the Prince of Peace will return and give peace to everyone who is infected with the word of peace; those who are rescued from their captivity to the devil."

"Nathan, I remember I was out there in the field with Dodo the Ahohite, He was a mighty man but the Philistines were so strong that they came at us and they surrounded us. All Israel ran away; they were scared. It was just the two of us who remained. We fought, yes we fought them; they faded. In the end when the Philistines were defeated, the people came back. Dodo's hand was stuck to the sword; it could not be separated. That was how long, how hard we fought. I defended his back and he defended mine and we fought."

"That is you, my king. You are always working, fighting, exerting, sweating, giving your heart, giving your all. Others would have given up; they would have been defeated. When the enemy raged, when their backs were against the wall, they would have given up but not you my king, you are a warrior, you fight, you have a mind-set to work. Just as with your heart to build the temple, you never give up until you die. You may not be able to do all you want to do but you will do all you can and apply all your energy to it. I wish every kingdom citizen was like you. My king, even when you are not on the battlefield, you are always on the field for battle, always in prayer, writing songs, building instruments, instructing your sons and especially your successor, Solomon. You have never taken one moment of your responsibility lightly, and my king, your heart and your attitude was not for you alone, it was never meant for you only, it is for every kingdom citizen. The time will come my king, I tell you, that the earth will see wars like never before but the wars are spiritual wars. It will happen in the time of the end when the people of God will be surrounded by enemies; demonic forces will rage against them. Things

will change overnight, economies will shift. The people of God must have this mindset of work; to lay it all out and place their heart all in, until all the sheep is gathered."
David laughed at that analogy. It was funny. He knew he would not sleep for days until all the sheep was were gathered. It took him back to the time he was a shepherd boy.

"Until all the sheep are gathered", Nathan repeated. "Until all the people that are to be saved are saved for the kingdom of God; until the harvest that is white and ready is fully reaped. The citizens of the kingdom who are safely in the kingdom must continue to work and to lay it all out until then. That is the mind that we all need."
David smiled, he understood very well what Nathan was saying. He himself had not just given everything for the kingdom and for the expansion and the peace of a kingdom, but he gave it all out for the quality of the kingdom. There is no kingdom that can enjoy or boast quality life without God. He did everything in his power to empower the priest and to empower the ministry ofto God; that was what the temple was all about. He wrote music and songs for the people and to God. He built instruments for them to use in worship. His life was about establishing the kingdom of God, not just his kingship. He recognized his responsibility as a responsible kingdom citizen first and so being king did not shift him or changed his responsibility, being king empowered him.

Aren't we all kings and priests, John thought, that should empower us, not shift our responsibility.

"You are an example for all kings to come in Israel" Nathan said. I tell you a secret David, you are an example for all citizens of the kingdom. God is about to do new thing and every person will become a king and a priest in their own right and you are an example of work, dedication, determination, love for God, pursuit of God, pursuit of the things of God, pursuit of the kingdom of God and making it your priority, putting it first, giving your heart soul and body to the very last to ensure the kingdom of God and the things of God, the heart of God in this earth is established. You are an example of the kingdom mind-set of work."

Nathan left but David knew that it would not stop with that conversation; he had work to do. God had restrained him from building the temple but he did not restrain him from building the people, he would invest in Solomon. He would tell him that above everything, to get wisdom and understanding. Wisdom begins with the fear of the Lord. That would sustain him, he would enforce it and ensure that he gets it in his heart. If he ever had a wish or a desire or a pursuit in life, he would pursue wisdom and understanding. He would also set the order for the priest to enter into the temple that was yet to be built. Perhaps God would see his heart and even give him the design for the temple.

DEPTH TILL DEATH

REPAYING THE DEBT OF LOVE

The grave the richest place indeed;
With buried visions; buried dreams
When love makes life a driving force
Then age will not abate its course
The energy slow but not the drive
The method, not the impact on lives
The depth is called up for the wise
To press beyond life's gift of time

You press on through succession
So your impact will live on
Beyond time and life's restriction
And your legacy remain

To the very end David worked. His heart was set to ensure that even after he passed he would have left a legacy for the people to follow and faithfully love his God. He drained his energy to ensure that the will of God and the heart of God was established in his nation and with his people. His passion was that the nation of Israel would not just have peace, but it would be positioned to serve God in every way possible.

John thought as he reflected on the life of David. "Is there anything different that God requires of us in this time?" He answered his searching heart, "No!"

Effectiveness requires work; there is no ending of the work so we work to the end and pass the legacy down. David's sin with Bathsheba is an example of what happens when kingdom citizens refuse to engage the work necessary. Refusal to engage is openness for attack. The devil does not accept a demilitarized zone. He does not relent because you have conceded or because you are not active, instead, he sees you as an easy target.

Isn't that why Paul said in Ephesians six. You are not fully armored until you have your feet shod with the preparation of the gospel of peace. You are not fully defended unless you are activated, unless you are going; unless you clothed yourself with the kingdom mind-set of work.

John went back to observe David. He was a prime example. His heart had on a temple for the Lord. He was not selected to fight in this battle but He would prepare Israel for victory. There is nothing more potent to secure victory for a nation than to culture the presence of the Lord and to nurture a healthy spiritual climate in the nation. He was very disappointed when, after initial agreement with his plan, the prophet Nathan returned with a message from God and restrained him. David would not be stopped; he was told the temple was approved but it would be built by his son Solomon. God understood the heart of David; it was full of God. God was everything to him and because of this, He gave him the architectural design for the temple. It was unique; like nothing ever built in his time. His son Solomon was to build the temple but David was not satisfied. He was not given the job as the builder but he could take the occupation as preparer.

He would occupy his time preparing. He would gain fulfillment to know he did everything he could to make it happen. He could not go but he could send, and if that was all he could do, he would give his heart, his strength and all his resources to it.

"There is always something to do for the kingdom of God," John chuckled. "It may not be what you want, but if you understand it is not about you, it will always be with all your heart. The one question to ask is, 'How will the kingdom benefit?'"

David's preparation was exceptional. The years leading to David's death saw the king busier than ever before. He had the plans so he knew the magnificence God was expecting and he gave it his magnificent best. His son would never wonder how to get started. David would give him a very good start.

"Is there any temple more magnificent in God's eye than a redeemed soul?" John thought aloud. "An earthly temple never makes it to heaven. Look what the Chaldees did to Solomon's temple." Is there any pre-occupation more important than building spiritual temples, saving lives? Is that not an assignment for everyone?

David prepared gold, he prepared silver

and he prepared timber. He organized the workers, singers, the musicians, and the Levites. That was something that he could do, and he gave himself to it. David prepared even to his death. In fact, after the Bible quoted some of the last words of David in 2 Samuel 23, he organized and structured the Levites, numbered them by house and designated them as gatekeepers, musicians and other service in the house of the Lord that was not yet built. He also numbered the priests and positioned them for service.

"Mmm," John thought. "Nothing stops you from giving your heart to whatever the Lord gives you the capacity to do. Nothing stops you from going all out even when you are all in; nothing stops you from winding out when your time is winding up. A kingdom mindset never quits.

The end of the book of 1 Chronicles captured the last days of David. He detailed his charge and designation for the temple workers, charged his son Solomon before everyone with the duty of building the temple and publicly handed over his store of offerings and provisions he had made for the temple.

The kingdom mindset never entertains retirement until death or complete incapacitation. Where you can work you give it everything; where you cannot work you impart, organize, empower, send and mentor. There will be more than enough time in glory to rest, but for now we labor until we enter there.

John smiled as he thought of his father. He had the kingdom mindset. He was dying of cancer and in extreme pain, but he would not go until John got this final revelation, the final impartation. He had taught John the ways of the kingdom and released his ministry to him, now he wanted to ensure he got in his spirit the attitude of the kingdom. John had come to discover the urgency, the attitude of work, and the priority kingdom demands. His father was in severe pain but he only allowed himself to sleep after John came by, day after day and talked to him about his research.

If you want to accomplish anything for God, you have to give your heart to it, you have to give yourself to it, you have to give yourself for it, you have to give everything into it and you never stop until your breath ceases, even when you are physically restrained.

If you want to get ahead then you have to get in, you have to get down and you have to get doing. The devil never sleeps; his demons are always active, always working.

There are people positioned on this earth to counteract Satan. The impact of many is muted by laziness. There is a generation to rescue and it will take more than just knowledge. It demands work. Father knows I am going to position my generation and do everything for them to get it. Knowledge without work is of no worth; it is worth less than its potential, or just simply worthless.

What did Jesus say? Jesus said, "I must work the work of God who sent Him while it is day for the night is coming when no one can work."

In other words, I must keep working until night, in full recognition that I have little time, or rather, no time. I must work eternity while times allows until I step into it, because eternity is very close.

Imagine you are dead...well not really! Perhaps caught up to meet the Lord. You are in your place of great comfort and you are looking over the great invisible gulf and seeing directly into that place of torment. Will it be sweet relief that you persevered? Will it be mixed with immense regrets when you look at all the people you were close to, people you knew very well, those you ate with, slept with, had fun with, exchanged gifts with, did business with; those you were employed to and whom you employed; your children and grandchildren; all those close to you whom you did not take the time to witness to because you were so busy. Busy with what? With life? Or because you were so busy enjoying them that you did not engage them? Now there they are, in that place of eternal punishment; suffering severe torment. How will you feel seeing them in their true reality? Failure to engage the kingdom mindset of work breeds severe regrets.

There is no unhappiness in heaven, just pure joy. Some will wear a crown of righteousness and some will shine like the stars, but I am sure many will have regrets. This will definitely be one of our greatest regret and disappointment, when we see the many we have lost because we did not engage them. The opportunity we have missed for Jesus because we did not take a workman-like approach to the salvation of souls.

John sighed as he thought about this. He had done a lot himself but he could see the many missed opportunities staring him in the face. This is the greatest lesson his father had taught him in his dying hours: the kingdom mind-set of work keeps you going even to the last breath, to death. You are never too old to have an impact. If you cannot give strength, then give your heart. Young men indeed dream dreams; the old men see visions. The old does have a part to play in defining and igniting the dreams of the young, just as David with Solomon. "Just as my dearest father is doing now with me," John whispered. We go in-depth till death repaying the debt of love we owe to the Lord Jesus Christ.

John's mind took him to Caleb. He could see him. He was an old man, eighty years old yet still very vibrant. His body had no option but to dance with his spirit, and his spirit was on fire. Joshua was dividing the land among the people after his hard work of conquest.

Johns sighed in acknowledgment, "It takes hard work to advance the kingdom."

Just then a thought crossed John's mind and he laughed heartily, "People are so enthralled with the sun standing still. That was faith beyond question. It still captivates the imagination of the young and the old when they think about it today." John chuckled even harder.

"They never see the truth," he thought. "Battle is work, physical exertion that leaves you totally exhausted after a day in the sun with only one mantra, 'Kill or be killed.'

Not one soldier could sit out the battle or rest; this could easily equate to a decision to sit out the rest of their lives.

Can you imagine, after a full day and you are totally exhausted, happy for the night, the sun is extended and you have to do it all over again. Many would have been praying for the sun to go down to get a reprieve and a little sleep. Day connotes work. Jesus said, 'I must work the work of Him who sent me while it is day.'

Joshua commanded the day to stand still to extend the work and cement the victory. Now combine this with them marching all night the night before. The sun standing still is captivating to the thoughts, but the reality of the human effort needed to capitalize on this great spiritual wonder is pure, painful and arduous work. John could see them...

THE SUN STANDS STILL

WONDER FOR MANY; WORK IN REALITY

Command you sun to stand still
Are you ready for the cost?
To push your body beyond limits
As it prolongs your war
Command your sea to stand still
But you must push ahead
And walk until it takes you
Into your wilderness

We like to speak of victories
The wonders of the signs
But these are tools to help you work
And empower you to fight
Surely signs will follow
But they are in the go
When you work His will they work for you
So you can do much more

Israel had made an erroneous covenant with the Gibeonites. The nations were angry with the Gibeonites who were themselves mighty warriors and wise. They knew how to choose their battles well. They gathered against them to fight. It was a confederate of mighty nations. The Gibeonites sent to Joshua for help. "Joshua, we need your help. We have a covenant with you. Please help us. The nations are gathered against us. They will wipe us out."

Joshua responded, "Armies of Israel, we march tonight."

This may have seemed to be Gibeon's battle but by reason of covenant it became theirs. This also was a unique opportunity to fight one battle and defeat multiple nations they would later have to engage. This was their mission. Just as covenant enlisted Israel in Gibeon's battle, covenant enlists us in the battle of souls, we have a blood covenant with Jesus, and covenant enlists God in our battles.

God spoke to Joshua and assured him of victory. The men of Israel were inspected. It was already dusk but they had no time to rest. They began marching. They marched all night. From time to time they could hear the scamper or flutter of animals they had woken from deep sleep as they marched through the dead hours of the night. Joshua was very determined. He understood that time is of essence when it comes to kingdom matters. The moon shifted position slowly as it inspected them from both sides. Foot, waist, head, then waist and foot. It was very detailed. It was in no hurry.

John said to himself, "We have to be prepared to deny ourselves sleep and march all night in the spiritual battlefield we engage. You catch the satanic forces unawares and in their devilish act."

The men were tired and some very sleepy but they marched on. "Nothing like believers who are strident in prayers in the night hours; who will deny sleep to attend to kingdom matters." Many of the men we completely exhausted. They would have gladly stopped and rested but Joshua would not allow it. Some closed their eyes as they walked.

They came upon the camp at day break and began to rout the army. The army fled. Not only did their night hours bring the element of surprise but they had enlisted divine help by their night time persistency. It is not advisable to face the day without conquering the night. God sent mighty hailstones from heaven which killed more men than the armies of Israel. The enemy was on the run and the night was coming. They had marched all night and fought all day. The problem is that the enemy would be able to hide and escape under the cover of darkness. The night is a place to fight spiritual battles, to march, but physical battles need all the senses and strength in exertion. Joshua did not hesitate. He commanded the sun to stand still so he could complete this victory. His men had marched all night and fought all day. They were exhausted but complete victory requires complete sacrifice. You fight recurring battles unless you are willing to press your advantage. It is not good enough to be satisfied with partial success. Unless you attain all the promises in the word to you, the sun must stand still while you rampage spiritual battlefields to claim what is yours. Unless you get a release in prayer don't get up. Let the hours pass while you press. This was Joshua's mentality. It is the Kingdom Mindset of Work. The body does not dictate your measure of success. It is a facilitator not an instructor. You dictate to the body. The body will have victories to enjoy for its cooperation. It will be severely attacked and perhaps wounded and destroyed if it refuses to fight. The kingdom demands people who are task-oriented, who will never relent until the flock is fully gathered; who will sweat for the kingdom with their last breath; who will forget comfort and embrace the contention for souls initiated on the cross; who will give it their strength, their hearts, their lives and their all; who fully understands the urgency of the times and fear the terror of the Lord on sinners.

Hmmm, John thought, it takes battle, hard work, blood and sweat to bring the kingdom to men, or to bring men into the kingdom.

Did the Bible not say, "You have not yet resisted to blood striving against sin"? There is an expectation that we give whatever it takes to ensure sin does not win in the lives of the people we love. The blood of Jesus and the cross are the symbols of our resistance and the template for our mindset of sacrifice.

John could see them on the battlefield; he could see them, weary, bruised, wounded, some dead. There are casualties of conflict, but this mindset is necessary to win what the Lord has given us.

If the Lord gives it to you, John thought, it does not mean you have it on a platter; you have to take it. There are so many promises in the word for the people of God. There are so many promises in the word and in the cross for sinners. The death of Jesus is the greatest promise for every person and the most lavish expose of the heart of God. Yet, until it is received, it is an unattained promise. Someone has to go, to take it, to share it. It will take work. A meaningful effort will take the mindset of work. Many will never obtain the promise or attain to glory unless there is a Caleb-mentality: ready to battle, ready to defeat satanic forces, ready to fight for souls and to rescue them.

The mind-set of work that the kingdom demands in today's age, is the same mind-set as in Joshua's days. It requires the same energy, the same blood-resistance, the same heart of sacrifice.

UNTIL ALL THE FLOCKS ARE GATHERED

There is no place for relaxation
on the battlefield
Your break or inaction
will deny heaven's yield
You cannot be contented
as if you are not bothered
There is no place of satisfaction
Until all the flock is gathered

Not because you are safe
Means you are to be satisfied
You can't secure yourself
When Jesus is denied
There is a rest for believers
But earth is not the realm
Let us labor therefore
So we may enter in

"There is no time to sit down and procrastinate." John thought as his mind took him back to the three tribes: Gad, Reuben and the half-tribe of Manasseh. These three tribes possessed their inheritance on the other side of Jordan before Israel crossed over. It was the land that they took from Og and Sihon.

They came to Moses and requested the land and he consented but charged them to fight on until all the tribes had inherited their promise from God.

This is captured in the introduction and quotes from Numbers 32 of the CWDS Bible:

INTRODUCTION SUMMARY
Your sins will always find you out,
So be conscious of the Lord;
He will give you your heart's desire
If you follow His commands.
Possess the gates of your enemies,
And much more by strength of hand,
But your sins will ever find you out,
if you do not battle on.

QUIOTES
You may inherit immediately but you may not rest until everyone inherits.
Your possession and wealth are not your rest; your rest is when everyone possesses.
Until all men are saved the work continues; there is no rest until everyone inherits.
Your sins will find you out if you put personal comfort above kingdom building, or if you rest in complacency because you are saved and secure.
Build your wealth, build your homes; build your families—build the kingdom.

As John reflected on all of this he lamented: The people of God today are willing to enjoy the benefits of salvation and the security that comes with it, but not willing to battle on until everyone has inherited. There is no rest for believers until all the flocks are gathered; until the Lord of our salvation fulfills His desire that none be lost but that everyone comes to a saving knowledge of Him. Until then we labor that we may enter into His rest.

Yes, it is ours; yes, we have it; yes, we are already Christians; yes, we are saved; yes, we are benefiting from kingdom citizenship, but we cannot be settled until all the others to whom the promise belongs have occupied and are settled.

~ ~ ~ ~ ~ ~ ~ ~ ~ ~ ~ ~ ~

John could see Caleb coming to Joshua. He was old but looking very good for his age. He was a gem among his generation. There was no other elderly man around except for Joshua.

Caleb came to Joshua and said, "Give me the land that God gave to me when we went up as spies and the others rebelled against God. The Anakims are there, yes, the giants, the same giants that frightened all Israel are still there. I am eighty years old but I am still vibrant. I still have the vim, the vigor, the vitality. God gave it to me and I am ready to go and take it as my possession.
(Not because God gives it to you means that the giants will automatically go, or that the devil will not stand against you, or that individuals will not shoot arrows at you; you must still have to fight for it.)

Caleb was prepared to go and take the land

at eighty years old, to defeat the giants that all of Israel were afraid of then. He was confident for God gave it to him. What God gives to you guarantees your help from above and success below. There are so many things that God gives to us but we must have the mind-set to take it. The battle continues.

No matter how old you are, a kingdom citizen never retires they re-fire. You may change your method but you never change your message or your mandate. There are so many opportunities to reach the world today because of technology and globalization. Many however chose to focus on their age, their pains and on what they have or do not have.

Caleb was different. John could see him and all his men going up; ascending into the mountain for the fight. The giants melted before Caleb as he went and he fought them. Angels fought with him because he was ready to fight with God. If Caleb had not taken that land, those giants would be a snare in the side of all Israel. Somebody had to take it. Age is no restriction. Caleb entered into this possession for his generation and their generations because he was prepared to fight to the end.

Kingdom citizens can no longer afford to think of themselves only, but must prepare for their generation and generations to come. We claim, we take, we conquer, we defeat the devil, we put down the enemy, we blaze trails, we train a generation so that our children will live in peace and have a better chance to survive in the **end times. Every person that is saved was a** potential weapon in the hands of the devil, now captured and converted to kingdom use.

What time do we have to do it? Now, while it is day. We have to clothe ourselves in a work mentality and approach the kingdom as any other job, knowing the reward is sure. The night is quickly approaching when no one can work. What time do we have to do it? As long as we are in time we have time. And just like my father, John thought, even to our dying breath.

There may be a word that we can give that will inspire; there must be compassion directed towards all the people who are flowing through the gates of hell. The world needs to be impressed with what you have bubbling inside you. The potency never dies even when your body decays; legacy lives on.

SOLOMON

SWEATING WISDOM

Solomon was distinguished
Not by wisdom but by work
The display of his wisdom
Was the product of his work
He worked the wisdom
He did not keep it in his heart
To conjure up the success
That we all are searching for

For the greatness of his wisdom
Is nothing to compare
With the Holy Spirit in us
That we all have today
The wisdom of the Highest
Work is wisdom that's defined
Solomon searched out knowledge
And worked the knowledge he acquired

Knowledge is information
Basic acquisition
Understanding is appropriation or
of appreciation (of the information)
Wisdom is application
Or simply working the information

To put it in plain words
Wisdom is simply 'Work'

John was excited. The more he researched the topics the more revelation he received, the more inspired he was about the kingdom, and the more convinced he was that every kingdom citizen needed to engage, to embrace, to adorn themselves with the attitude of work to be an effective kingdom citizen.

He took an early night; he was tired. He tried to sleep but he could not. His thoughts on Solomon were beginning to excite him so much that it prevented him from sleeping.

"Solomon accomplished so much," John thought, "so much."

A response came back from his thoughts, "He was special, so very special. God separated him and distinguished him in leadership and made him very successful.

He is no different from us," John thought, we can do that too. Oh yeah, God gave Solomon the opportunity to ask anything that he desired, anything. Solomon had a distinct advantage, there is no way we can accomplish what he did or anything in comparison...or is there?

Did you say, ask anything? Did not Jesus say we are joint heirs together with Him? Did He not say ask anything and I will do it? Ask for whatever you desire and I will do it, that the Father may be glorified in Me.

What did Solomon ask for?

For an understanding heart.

Why?

So he could rule the people of God.

Well, what did James say?

He said you do not have because you do not ask, and you ask and do not receive because you make baseless requests that you may consume it on your own personal lust. Your motive is not right. What scripture is that again? Yes, James 4:2-3.

Oh, didn't Jesus say that, 'Whatever you ask the Father in My name I will do it.' Also, 'Ask and you will receive that your joy may be full.'

And if you say, 'But God said to David, "I will make of him a son." Solomon had special treatment, he was treated as a son of God.'

Aren't we sons of God by faith in Christ Jesus? Solomon was elevated to a place that we all are today."

John's thoughts kept going back and forth, justifying Solomon and negating it. He came to a realization that Solomon had nothing that we as believers do not have today.

He could hear Jesus say to his disciples and to those around him, that there has never been a person born of woman greater than John the Baptist. He was speaking of all the prophets and great men, whether Moses or Abraham, Isaac, Jeremiah, David or Solomon.

After saying this, He qualified it... and what a statement. He said the least in the kingdom of God is greater than John. In other words, Solomon was not greater than John the Baptist in spite of his accomplishments, but we are

John the Baptist proclaimed and ushered in a new era, this era. We live in the era of the Lord

Jesus Christ himself, the King of kings and the Lord or lords who baptizes with fire. John ushered in the era of the Holy Spirit. He said, the least in the kingdom of God irrespective of where we are or what we do, are greater than John the Baptist, who himself was greater than Solomon.

Does that mean Solomon does not have a distinct advantage over us?

Could it be, Solomon received understanding and wisdom to get wealth but he did not have the Holy Spirit living in him?

Now that makes us today a distinction.

So what is the difference? Why is it that Solomon accomplished so much and yet in today and in this generation we accomplish so little?

John began to think of it. What could have accounted for this? All he could see was the kingdom mind-set of work that Solomon applied to everything that he received.

John was transported back in his thoughts to the days of Solomon. He saw Solomon there; he was working.

~ ~ ~ ~ ~ ~ ~ ~ ~ ~ ~ ~ ~

"I have the plans that David my father gave me for the temple. It is so amazing, the level of detail that he documented and the store of treasure that he prepared. This temple is going to be exceedingly magnificent. I can see it; I have so much more preparation to do."

Solomon got busy immediately, organizing. He held meetings; assigned his captains and his delegates. He had individuals assigned by ranks for all functions. He had things structured and organized to the minute detail. Every aspect of the building of the temple and his kingdom was organized and supervised and assessed to satisfaction. From the cutting of stones, to the preparation, to the bringing of logs, to supplies and gold. It was a lot of work but it was personally supervised by King Solomon. The building of a temple required work. The building of the kingdom of God requires structure, organization and work.

John chuckled. "Aren't we all building a temple? Are we not the spiritual temple of God? Did not God say to Solomon that if they defiled the temple he built, He was going to destroy it? Didn't He eventually cause the Chaldeans and the Babylonians to totally destroy the temple Solomon built because it was defiled?

Isn't it the same thing that God says to us, "Your body is the temple of the Holy Spirit, if you defile the temple I will destroy it"?

All spiritual things in life requires a kingdom mindset. It is about building. It is about organizing ourselves and giving ourselves to the pillars of our spiritual life so that our temple will be standing and glorious in the sight of the living God.

Then the thought came to John: "Solomon was given the kingdom. Yes, he was made a son of God by God Himself and he was given a kingdom. He had an advantage."

His thoughts returned to correct him, "No, we have the advantage. God has made us all kings and priests, he has given us the kingdom.

Jesus came and He brought to us the kingdom of God. Solomon was given the kingdom of Israel. Our kingdom is even greater because it is spiritual; its domain is over Israel and all the earth. Solomon had the responsibility to tend the kingdom, to make his kingdom glorious for the people of God and for the God of his people. His first task was to build a temple, to ensure that the people were connected to their God. The greatest memorial of any kingdom is its spirituality. Everyone who saw what was done in Solomon's kingdom invariably pointed to the God of his kingdom.

When the queen of Sheba came, she saw organization, she saw structure, she saw order, she saw beauty, she saw the work that was done and established, she saw the lions that led up to the throne, she saw the people and the order with which they ate and this amazed her; she saw Solomon's God.

The queen of Sheba saw work, and the result of work. Solomon was given a kingdom but he worked what he was given. He was made a son of God and he worked it. **It takes work for what we are given and what we carry, to manifest.** God said that the least in the kingdom of God is greater than John the Baptist who is greater than Solomon. It means that what we are given is potential. Ask and I will give to you. God gave Solomon potential but Solomon worked it to abundance and extravagance.

Solomon was a man of work. It was not the wisdom that he was given that caused all the kings to come to him to hear what he had to say.

It was the wisdom he put on display; the knowledge he possessed; the knowledge he sought and applied that placed the wisdom on demonstration.

Is there any greater wisdom that exists than the wisdom that we all have today; the Holy Spirit who lives inside of us? Is He not the source and the seat of all wisdom? How many of us work the wisdom in us until it defines us; until people come to us because of the manifest presence of the Holy Spirit in us?

Solomon said in Ecclesiastes 2, "I applied my heart to know, to search and to seek out wisdom and the reason for things."

He also said, "I make my work great, built myself houses, planted vineyard, gardens and orchards, planted all kind of fruit trees, made water pools to water the trees, acquired male and female servants. In other words, I worked the wisdom and the wisdom worked for me; I had greater possessions than anybody in Jerusalem before me because I worked the wisdom.

I gathered; I sought; I acquired. These are all verbs. Solomon detailed how he took action and then he displayed results. I gathered silver and gold, special treasures of kings and provinces. I acquired all types of singers, delighted men and so I became great and excelled. Solomon was very clear that what he got from God was not greatness. What he got was the ability to attain greatness. He received the power to get wealth; the empowerment to overcome and be distinguished. He had to apply work to the seed of wisdom and understanding to produce wealth and greatness. He had to set his heart to do it.

God never gives to us the end product. He gives us the ability to do whatever he has assigned us to do: to reach nations, to touch people, to build His kingdom here on earth, to change lives, to get wealth, to live holy, to command angels, to trod upon serpents and scorpions, to live in divine health, yes, to build a sanctuary for His people to point them towards the living God. He has given us the ability to show people Jesus, to touch the lives of millions all over, to access everything that He has, kingdom resources for kingdom purposes. The flesh, however, ask for gifts in futility, that is, to acquire from heaven to consume on self and personal lust. The flesh desires to make itself comfortable in this world rather than to effect its assignment to impact this comfortable world; the lives of others. Heaven cries, "Heaven's resources for the kingdom purposes; ask and be empowered to satisfy the Father's heart; yes, for people." The flesh cries, "Heaven's resources for my heart, comfort. "The flesh's reality is that it is made of material that fades away and it lives in a world that fades away. Eternity investment cannot be flesh; it is eternal: spirit.

Jesus gave us the command to go, and with that command He released all things that we need for life and for Godliness. He gave us the Holy Spirit, who has all knowledge. We have full access to the resources of the Holy Spirit, unlike Solomon who was limited to physical resources and human wisdom, even the best of it. We have access to spiritual things; we have prophetic ability; we have God's ability; we are sons of God who can impact both the physical and the spiritual realm in these end times.

What Solomon got from God that day was the ability. What we have is the same ability with an unlimited resource, the Holy Spirit. What Solomon had, that God saw, was the mind-set of work and the willingness to invest that ability. He had the readiness to acquire knowledge so he could apply the understanding and produce manifest wisdom. Understanding is nothing without information. What else would you apply it to? Solomon pursued knowledge.

The kingdom mind-set of work in these end-times requires us to set our hearts to search the scriptures; to study to gain God's approval for heaven's release. To meditate in the scriptures so we can mediate the sacrifice of the cross. It requires us to set our hearts to apply the knowledge. Knowledge is power; the fear of the Lord is manifest power. It is the beginning of wisdom; it places the eye of the Lord on you. You set your heart to understanding spiritual things so that you can be kept away from the evil of these times; so that God may entrust kingdom resources to you and that you may be a blessing. You set your heart to be a blessing to the kingdom so that the kingdom may be established in the hearts of men. To be kingdom-minded you set your heart to do everything that the Lord Jesus has commanded. To go, to be active, to impact, to invest the talent the Lord has given you that all men will see your good works and glorify your Father in heaven. It does not matter what you have. Many people have been given things of great value and have allowed them to lie dormant. Some have lost it because of their negative works or lack of work. Work adds value to value as with Solomon.

Solomon received the kingdom of David, very valuable in his time. David had defeated kings and he took their wealth. Solomon added value to value. Because of the knowledge he acquired and the understanding and wisdom demonstrated, kings came and brought their wealth to Solomon instead of him going to war to get it as with David.

We are fighting a spiritual battle in this time. We are not engaged in physical fights. We are tearing down strongholds; we are building a spiritual kingdom, yet it requires physical exertion and sacrifice, both on the knees and in going. We are in battle and just like Solomon we have everything that we need but we have to engage it, we have to embrace it, we have to clothe ourselves in the kingdom mind-set of work in order to execute it. We must be ready to work what we have to the glory of God.

PAUL THE WORKAHOLIC

It was midday. John was in his office but he could do nothing but meditate on his revelations of the past days. It was resting heavily on him. He had examined the work attitude of Paul and his adrenaline was pumping. Paul was extraordinary but he was stewarding the ordinary gospel committed to everyone. His distinction was his work ethics.

As John contemplated how he would share these exiting revelations to his father later that day he turned it over in his heart.

"Dr. John, Reverend John!"

John looked up. He snapped out of his thoughts in that moment as he saw his secretary trying to get his attention.

"Ahh, John thought, that was a productive time at work. She probably thought I was day-dreaming. No, I was life-dreaming, or rather, preparing to begin my life all over. I am created for a life of effectiveness and I shall manifest."

"Yes, Sister Grace, how may I help?"

"It is about your father, Papa, He is asking to see you."

"What, is something wrong!"

John thought it very strange that his father should ask for him. He would normally wait patiently until John came to see him at his usual time in the evening.

"Nothing that I know of sir. His nurse did not communicate an emergency. Just that he is asking to see you."

As he thought about his father, he said to himself, "Dad wants nothing more than to leave with an attitude of pursuit that compels success. He desires to inject a generation with passion through me. Indeed, the mind-set of every kingdom citizen should be a mind-set of work that never shifts with age; instead the urgency intensifies as the time gets shorter."

John got up immediately. He closed his door and hurried to his car. He did not notice that he was literally running. He turned the key and set out for his father's side. Unconsciously he knew it was unusual for him to be called at this hour. He did not notice that his foot was a little heavy on the accelerator. He did not notice members of the congregation waving to him from under the breadfruit tree. He did not notice the police car until he passed them and heard the siren. He looked at his speedometer as he pulled over and realized he was 10kpm over the limit. He heard himself explain that he must have been a little anxious, being summoned by his father at this time of the day. His father was well known and the officer was a member of his vast congregation. He was allowed to proceed with a warning and a word of caution.

He was more conscious of his surrounding as he proceeded prayerfully along the last few kilometers. He did not notice how hard he pushed the door of his father's room until he heard it slam on the wall and saw everyone startled. He noticed the smile on his father's face to welcome him as the nurse stepped out. He felt a rush of relief as he waited for his father to speak.

"John, my son," his father said, painfully. Your work has pleased me so well. I have been so inspired by you that I feel I could rise from this bed and apply some of the principles today."

John laughed. He was still laughing when his father said, "What did you learn about Paul."

John was ready. He began by quoting 1 Corinthians 11 from verse 22. He observed the broad smile cover his father's face as he read. It was self-explanatory.

"In labors more abundant, in stripes, much more than one person should receive; I lived in prisons; I have been incrassated so many times; in death-defying situations often. From the Jews I received thirty-nine stripes five times. I was beaten with rods three times and pelted with stones; I suffered shipwreck three times and spent a day and a night in the deep sea. I was moving up and down spreading the gospel all the time. My life was always in danger at sea and on the land from robbers and my own people. I put my life at risk among the nations I witnessed to. I was in danger in the wilderness, at sea, in the city and among false brethren. I tirelessly toiled, often without sleep and exhausted; hungry and thirsty many times and fasting was my way of life. I was in the cold, sometimes I had nothing to wear.

In addition to this, I was daily concerned about the churches. Was there anyone weak and I was not weak, or any made to stumble and I was not irked?

Paul's life was a summary of a kingdom work attitude. His success and longevity throughout Christian history was not handed to him as a portion in life. He had the same conversion as we all have; the same Holy Spirit anointing but he set his heart to work."

John paused, but his father waved him on. He wanted to hear everything that was in John's heart. There was an extra urgency and enthusiasm today.

"Daddy," John said. "Paul has blown away any excuse a kingdom citizen may give not to work, to be effective or to achieve.

Solomon says, 'The lazy man says there is a lion in the streets, I will be eaten; or it is too cold. They turn on their hinges like a door while their kingdom deposit lies idle growing weeds and thorns.'

Paul said we worked harder than everyone else. It means that everyone may determine the measure of their work and dictate the measure of their success. He placed all in and went all out. In the process, he blew away the excuse of personal hardship, personal pain, personal danger, personal safety and self-preservation.

Beatings came and he took it again and again to maximize the kingdom deposit in him; prison came and he outlasted it; he outlived attempts at his life to get the gospel out.

He persisted through the highs and the lows,
through the heat and the cold,

through hunger and thirst,
shipwrecked and much worse,
through the stones pelting flesh,
battered and left for death,
he got up and with his next breath;
he preached Jesus still;
For the gospel cannot be killed.
It takes a mindset of work
To truly get the gospel out;
Though Satan will be irked,
And will fight your every move.

Paul ensured that while his body suffered, the gospel he carried was protected. It was not allowed to be beaten out of him; stoned, starved, drowned, imprisoned, in fact his imprisonment only set it free and extended its life through letters.

Papa, I can see him in the ocean. The angry waves dashing at him; the raging sea threatening his continued existence and relevance. The waters went over his head time and again as he hung to a piece of the boat and swam towards the shore. A surge came and knocked the wind from him and he fought. There were others fighting: the captain, the crew and others, prisoners, oh yes he was a prisoner also.

I can see him moments later, totally exhausted and lying flat, catching his breath on the shore while the villagers gathered around him. They expected that at least one, if not many of those who made it to shore would be bodies, but they were all alive. It was the grace upon this man to preserve life. It was not long after this before he was ministering to the entire island.

Papa, I can see him on another occasion, in the midst of a deep angry sea. He was holding to fragment of another boat as the wave rocked him like a ragged doll. The clouds looked angrily at him as if energized by demonic forces that opposed him. The sea churned around him as if stirred up by the marine kingdom's synchronized dance. He held on for his life. He had no time to think about the dangerous sea and what may be lurking in the waters. As the waves rocked him, all he could think about was the people that he had to reach in Antioch and the people that he still had to reach in Corinth. He had a certain peace within him because of the work. For to him, to live was Christ, or rather work, living for Christ. He was out there a day and a full night. He could not afford to sleep and have his float of ship fragment drift away from him. It was exhausting. The following morning, he was rescued. Only God knows what kept this man going because he was shipwrecked not one time, not two times, but three.

I can see him daddy, on Malta on that final shipwreck. Coming out of the peril of the sea and the death that everyone had resigned to. The villagers were very kind, extremely kind. They prepared food and took care of all who came ashore, the prisoner and the crew alike. Paul was there grabbing some wood to put on the fire. He had an attitude to work; to help in any way he could. A very poisonous serpent latched onto his hand. He shook his hand so it fell into the fire. They expected him to die but he did not die. A peril of death twice escaped in just one instance yet he kept going, witnessing to the villagers, telling them about Jesus. All that was on his heart was the kingdom, translated as work. He healed many, from the household of the chief to many villagers who came to him. He kept working, caring, forgetting about his own circumstance even though he was a prisoner and he was being taken to judgment. Does the kingdom mind-set of work give any reason or any cause for an excuse? Certainly not for Paul! Unfortunately, many kingdom citizens today conclude otherwise. They are cast out by the sea of trials as useless firewood instead of living stones.

We have an order for our King to work. He said to go. He also said the fields are white, ready for harvest. It communicates urgency and a harvest that can be spoilt in the field. He committed us all to pray that God will send laborers. The irony is that we all have the Holy Spirit and we all carry the kingdom. Must it take prayer to commit believers, including ourselves, to work? Some are mobilized, yet many more give excuses as they pursue life in the kingdom and not the life of the kingdom or the pleasure of the King. Paul gave and accepted no excuse for himself. Not by his body, not by his circumstances, not by anything. In fact, once he excused his weary followers to take a boat while he walked on foot so he could maximize the ministry opportunity.

Papa, can you believe that with all this he engaged his trade in order to provide for himself on the mission field? He excused lack as an excuse and believers who were stingy with kingdom resources. Nothing should hinder his mission if work was a solution.

I can see him, Papa, his back tattered; thirty-nine lashes with a cat o' nine whip. The metal at the end of that whip tearing into his back, the flesh coming out and the blood all over the place, all because of his attitude towards work; all because he did not see danger as an excuse. In fact, for him the lives of men and the souls of men were worth the sacrifice. This did not happen one time, otherwise we could brush it off and perhaps, by association, bring up something that occurred to us even though it may not have been as brutal. It did not happen two times nor three times nor four times, but all of five times. Paul kept going. He had work to do and to do the work, he would accept no excuse, not from his weary legs, not from his tattered flesh.

If this was not enough, I can see him, beaten with rods, thick boughs of branches meant to batter him. He accepted this three times. I can see him. His bloody body resembled nothing like his strident spirit; glowing gloriously even more every day.

I can see him Papa; they had just stoned him and left him for dead. They expected him not to rise again. He had stopped breathing, in fact, that may have saved his life. As the brethren gathered around him and grieved expecting a funeral service, he rose up. That should have been enough of an excuse not to go on: it is too dangerous, too perilous, but for Paul there would be no excuse. Immediately, he got up and went into the city to encourage the brethren and moved on to preach in another city.

What can be our excuse Papa?

It cannot be money, Paul suffered lack. He understood that the vision was his from God; provision was God's for His vision. It cannot be that we are too tired or too worked to pray. Paul was in weariness and toil and many nights he did not sleep. We are not talking about a scheduled prayer time of twelve to five or three to six or one to three or whatever time in the night we choose to pray; he did not sleep. He spent twenty-four hours praying and working. While we encourage rest, it must be built around fulfillment and not otherwise. He moved from place to place recognizing the urgency of the times and the times of urgency of the gospel.

Jesus needs people who will avenge the cross and avenge His death by keeping His work alive. People who will give everything for others to gain and to enter the kingdom.

Paul was hungry many times and thirsty many times when he was not fasting, yet he fasted many times when he was full, rather constantly. He needed food that hands could not provide. He was cold many times, naked without clothes many times, yet he served the Lord. In addition to those who lay-waited to rob him for he travelled dangerous roads, he faced arrows from false believers. This is an emotional battle that hurt the most but could not derail his message.

He also cared for the churches, he prayed for believers, he felt weak when they were weak. He pursued his mission in the flesh and on his knees. He even commanded believers to pray without ceasing and told us that the attitude of overcoming in pursuit of mission is to give thanks in everything. For Paul, it was a manner of life.

Papa, this is what Christianity is all about. We are in the kingdom but we have to engage that mindset of work, recognizing that what Jesus did was to establish a template. This template is given to believers to ensure that His kingdom is established in the earth; that His death is avenged. That His will that none be lost has expression through our lives. That no harvest will spoil in the field; none will die in sin who we have the ability to reach. We have to make His mandate personal and set our hearts to His field. Our hearts must pump and bleed, not with our own concerns but with Him. Jesus debunked selfish living. He said, "Seek first the kingdom and I will take care of your concerns. I am able, I have done it for the flowers of the field and I have done it for the birds of the air in an extravagant way."

When we care about what concerns Him, He actively cares about what concerns us.

THE RACE

A RACE REQUIRES A RUN (ENERGY)

You: sluggish, lethargic, lackluster
Lukewarm, lazy, languid
Relaxed, leisurely, languorous
Unhurried, indolent, sluggish, insipid
Surprise! Got news, so come awake
The Christian walk is an active race
Assert, exert, no time to waste
New attitude; now change your pace

To follow you take up your cross
Your blood and sweat the greatest cost
Work sculptures the footprints of Christ
Passion will ensure you're not left behind

"**P**apa, Paul saw the Christian walk as a race. He said, everyone who runs a race run the race set before them with endurance. Also that many run in a race, but not everyone receives the prize. To gain the prize, you must clothe yourself with the mindset to run and run in such a way to obtain it. There is a way to run to have victory; there is a fervency, there is a level of preparation, there are rules that you have to abide by in order to win. Paul spoke about his own race, he said, 'I run, not with uncertainty. I know what I am doing and I don't fight as one who beats the air. I am deliberate. I refuse to run and to know that I have run in vain.'

In another scripture, he says, 'I hold fast the word of life that when Christ comes I can rejoice so I have not run or labored in vain'.

In his letter to the Hebrews chapter twelve, he says, 'Let us run with endurance the race that is set before us.'"

"Papa," Peter also said, "They think it strange and unusual, that you do not run with them in the same dissipation, doing all the evil that they do."

Everybody is running. Life is like a race and we are all running. We all exert energy all the time, but are we expending the energy on the right things?

Paul also sees the kingdom mind-set of work as a fight, he says "Fight the good fight of faith."

Either way, whether a race or a fight we exert energy, both in preparation and execution. A fight takes intense and extreme energy, even to exhaustion. Paul did say the good fight of faith. There are things that we fight for in life: for scarce benefits, for our lives, for things that will satisfy us temporarily, we exert energy, so much energy in taking care of our own selves that we have little time for the things of God.

These are fights but there is a good fight. It is the fight of faith, the fight for the souls of men. Paul commits us all to this fight.

Paul says, "I do not fight as one who beats the air."

In another chapter, he urged Timothy again to fight the good fight of faith, and to lay hold on eternal life.

It is obvious Papa, that not because we are saved means that our salvation is secured, and not because we are saved means that we are maximizing what the Lord has deposited in us. The kingdom requires all believers to engage a mind-set of work, a mind-set of fight to survive and to maximize.

Paul later charged Timothy in his first epistle to him, to fight the good fight of faith and to wage the good warfare."

He also told believers, "I have fought the good fight, I have finished the race, I have kept the faith."

He also referenced fighting, in Ephesians 6. He told the Ephesians to put on the entire armor of God. We have to embrace the fighting mentality and keep on the entire armor of God at all times. Whether we fight or not we are in a battle and the enemy does not care what our readiness is. He will never stop fighting. We will either lose our souls or cause the souls of others to be lost on this battlefield if we refuse to fight, to work.

Because Jesus gave His life for the world, it is called the good fight. It is a fight to retain and distribute what Jesus died for. We have to use spiritual tools to tear down all those walls and bars that are being placed around them, and to deliver to them the kingdom of God that belongs to them. A heavy price was paid; the price of blood, but the package must be delivered. The kingdom mind-set in this time will require work. In these end times, the demonic opposition will be greater, even greater than ever before. We are in the times of darkness and those who are not fighting and those who are lazy will be thrown into the battle in ways they can never imagine. Witchcraft is on our doorsteps and in our households; satanic worship is in our squares and demons are getting legal permission to our nation and communities. More than ever before, for the church to rise and remain relevant, for believers to survive, we have to take a militant approach to our faith. If the enemy advances, the church is on the run, or on the back foot, if Christians advance, the devil is on the run. The answer is in our fight and our attitude of work."

John saw his father's eye light up at his authoritative and aggressive response to the urgency we currently face in these times. John was no more a student sent on an assignment of discovery; he was now the teacher.

As John continued, there was a certain release and radiance on his father's face.

"Yes, our head has to be covered but our feet must also be shod with the preparation of the gospel of peace. We have to take the gospel. The demand was met but the need did not end at Calvary; it requires the mobilization of a Jesus force. It is not just us celebrating what happened at Calvary for us, but to cause others to celebrate also. We have to give it to them! We have reach them and invite them into this great inheritance," John was forceful.

John thought about the life of Paul. "I can see Paul papa. He is there preaching and sharing the gospel to the very end. I see him looking for opportunities even while in prison, bringing the people to him. He could not go but they came. He invited them. He witnessed while he was being accused. He talked about Jesus even when it angered the people he spoke to. He was consistent, constant, and his life is memorable. The stories of his life, his walk, his testimony and the letters he wrote are inspirational.

Papa when he was imprisoned, he wrote so others could benefit from the knowledge and experience he acquired; the things that the Lord had deposited in his spirit. No, his ministry did not end with his imprisonment; he ministered to the very end.

Papa, every person can make an impact but it takes a mind-set of work. We all have what Solomon had, a template. In fact, we have a greater platform. We all have been asked to do it, and many have the heart to do it but unless we engage the task to do it, it reaches nowhere; an unmarked to do list. It does not matter how great we are or how much knowledge or skill we have; it does not matter what the Lord has deposited in us. Even the immensity of what He deposited in Solomon needed the propensity of his work; for nothing works unless we work it. This applies to the best of equipment and also to the anointing. Solomon sent to get gold from Ophir. The knowledge that there was gold in Ophir was not enough. The fact that it was accessible did not fill his treasuries. He had to build ships and send men to mine it. He had to build relationship. He had to gain knowledge and work the knowledge. The fact that there is gold in every heart and a potential Christ in everyone does not make them all believers. We have to work that knowledge. Papa, for Paul it was the same. He had a unique experience with the Lord, but we cannot discount our own experiences. It was the Holy Spirit that made him effective. The same Spirit is in every believer."

John, was preaching to himself as he thought about the life of Paul. He saw him beheaded, his body convulsing with the last throngs of death. His head was on the ground a few meters away. "With his last breath he delivered," John whispered. "With his last breath." It was barely audible but his father heard and sighed, "With my last breath."

John could see them. The many the enemy has engaged with distractions. Gadgets, games, movies and other time-wasters. His aim is to de-weaponize us as the Philistines did to Israel. He uses little toys, perversion, movies and other things to distract and poison. In the days of King Saul, the Philistines ensured there were no swords in Israel. They had a plan to win without a fight. The enemy continues this strategy to make us ineffective in the spiritual world while he attacks us, our families and others.

"We have to reengage a kingdom mind-set of work," John sighed as he broke the silence of his reflections. "A man who fights does not entangle himself with the affairs of this world. Isn't that another quote from the apostle Paul?"

~ ~ ~ ~ ~ ~ ~ ~ ~ ~ ~ ~

John looked at his father and sat quietly. His father was coiled up with a strange look of satisfaction on his face, yet he looked so weak and frail... so frail.

"Noooo!"

A RACE WELL RUN

THE PASSING OF THE BATON

Hang on to the moment and think that it will last
The ones who ran before you ran so well, so much impact
Let go of the moment; you have no time to bask
Their race in now ended; the baton has been passed
You honor them by building on the foundation they raised
By the greater works projected, put their impact on display
More energy, more impact; apply sweat to the seeds sown
For the baton is with you; and the race is now your own

These moments would follow John for life as he recounted them.

He had just finished sharing with his father his revelations on Paul. He had taken a seat observing his father's reaction. His father was coiled up with a strange look of satisfaction on his face, yet he looked so weak and frail... so frail. Etched in his memory was that certain glory all over his father as he had passionately shared with him progressively all the things that he had been meditating on and all the discoveries that he made, even in this research. There was a certain sense of accomplishment when he saw the passion in John's eyes for his generation and for believers to understand that the kingdom demanded work. He remembered the chuckle that came to his father's lips once. It was quickly erased by the pain, but the smile of satisfaction was always there.

John looked at him now and there was this indescribable gleam in his eyes. His eyes closed as at other times, as if to sleep. He opened it again and briefly looked up at John and said, barely audible, "Jesus, I see Jesus." His eyes closed again.

John thought he was sleeping. He remained for a few minutes to be sure. It was then he noticed there was no breath. Immediately he panicked and called for the nurse. The nurse came rushing in. She checked his pulse, there was none. The doctor came minutes later and John was placed out of the room. It was not long before the news was confirmed. His father had passed on.

Tears came to John's eyes and rushed down his face. He could not help it, even when he remembered the gleam of satisfaction he saw in his father's eyes at the end and his last words. He knew his father was fulfilled. He had fought a good fight. He had got the sendoff he desired. A final impartation to his son and successor whom he sent on a mission of discovery.

John cried, he could not help it. He knew he would be crying for days. He broke when he received the news.

His father, a stalwart in the kingdom, a man who worked hard, who established many ministries, who fathered many sons, who blessed and released many in his time, is dead. He left John a hard road to follow and extra-large shoes to fill.

In his dying moments with the doctor's decree on his life, he found strength and energy to prolong his days. He felt the need to impart to John a mind-set of work that would remain and make him effective in his mandate. It would also become his mandate to impart this revelation to his world so they would not just hear it but live it. John knew his father had prepared, positioned and equipped him to prepare his world for the end times.

"Daddy died with a smile on his face, a gleam in his eyes, calling on Jesus," he said, consoling himself.

~ ~ ~ ~ ~ ~ ~ ~ ~ ~ ~ ~ ~

"Why did he call on Jesus," John thought, "was he seeing Jesus or did he feel fulfilled that he had accomplished what Jesus wanted him to do?

Well perhaps..." John thought. "Could it be...

Could it be that he wanted me to take a look at the life of Jesus and His mind-set for work?"

Either way, John knew there was no way for him to close this research without looking at Jesus Himself and His mind-set towards work. Jesus is the one who created the template on which we build. He Himself was the template of work; He worked. He Himself was the object, the instructor, the instruction and the instrument of the work needed in these end times.

Although his father would not be around to listen to this final chapter of his research, John knew he owed it to his father to complete it and to put the instructions and revelation to work.

John would bury his father, but he would find relief from the pain of his death, in looking at the life of Jesus, and reviewing his father's mandate to him, to work. This is what his father lived for and as long as he continued it, his father would live on through him.

"I will never let Papa die," John committed to himself, as his thoughts centered on Jesus. Rather I stubbornly refuse to let Jesus die in vain. He lives on with all His passion and energy in me. I will certainly study Him. Did He not say, "Take My yoke (burden for the world; attitude of work; compulsion to arduous servitude) on you and learn of me..."

A NEW DAY

EYES AWAY FROM MAN; SEE JESUS

John sat on a swing in the park. He was devastated. It was a week after his father's funeral and he could do little. It was difficult to concentrate or work. The pain was too much. He loved his father dearly. Not only was he a perfect example in ministry but he was a family man; he spent time with John. He was never too busy to listen to John, to give him personal time, to take him out to play and to play with him. He would instruct him with such a measure of gentleness that John felt that life without him was not life. John knew he had to let him go, he was old and John had his own responsibility, his own family, but even then the pain was so much, too much.

He remembered his father's last word, "Jesus", and John began to think of what his father could have meant. He knew in his final days he had instructed him to research the kingdom mindset of work displayed by successful persons in the Bible. It was a mission of discovery. His father had done it in his own classical style, all the lessons he had for John, he had found a way to get John to discover it himself. John himself had a charge. He had people he was responsible for. He had the churches his father had established and networks his father had led for him to continue. He had this great revelation that he received in his research that he had accepted as the instructions to him from his father. His father needed to pass it on in a way that it would become lifestyle. Now the pain was intense but every time he thought about Jesus it was alleviated. Something was propelling him to finish his research. It brought his father to life again.

In his meditation he realized that everything that he had researched so far came together in Jesus; everything was fulfilled in and centered on Jesus.

A DAY IN THE LIFE OF JESUS

THE TEMPLATE FOR WORK

"I have been at this for some time," John said to himself, "and I cannot find a day in Jesus' life that is not filled with determination, focus and work."

I can see them:

The sun was high in the sky, compelling attention with its piercing heat. John could see Jesus and His disciples. They were walking. They had been walking now for hours. The dust from the streets covered their sandals and baked onto their feet. Jesus wiped the sweat from His brow as He looked compassionately at the small crowd that had followed Him. He traveled from one place to another on foot as He had no other means of transportation. At times He would walk miles just to spread the gospel of the kingdom. At times the crowd pressed against Him and gave Him no time for rest or personal relief. They called out their need to Him constantly. Ministry is work but it is a work of love. You must embrace the work to extract the worth.

If the work ethics of Jesus could be summed up in a poem, perhaps the poets would write:

Did cower from the hot sun?
Did He wait for men to come?
What was His means of transport?
Did He not walk from town to town?

The answer to these words was obvious Jesus had no areophane, no tents, no air-conditioned auditoriums, no motor cars and red carpets; hotel conference rooms for privileged audiences. If ministry could be rough, Jesus roughed it every day until ministry roughed Him up and eventually took His life.

The pen of the poets would continue the inquisition with more searching questions:

Was He ever without a multitude following?
Was He ever without the crowd?
When He sought a private moment they sought Him
No rest with them around.
Was He ever in the comfort
Of a cozy bed to sleep?
Did He ever have a place to lay His head?

THE BURDEN OF THE CROWD

A MAJOR WEIGHT OF MINISTRY

John could see Jesus, or rather could hardly see Him without a crowd. They followed Him everywhere like scavengers, wanting to draw from the grace He carried. "O that people today would be this hungry," he thought.

It was evening. The dust arose from the streets with the wind and coated everyone on the street. Today the streets were unusually crowded. People came from everywhere. The news about this Teacher was the talk of the town, or rather, every town and the entire country and countries surrounding Israel. People came from everywhere.

When there is a move of the Holy Spirit by a person willing to tap it, you will realize how much people need solutions.

If you are locatable they will locate you.

If you are available, they will come to you.

If you are findable they will find you.

If you are resting they will find you.

If you are busy; they will increase your load.

They do not come to seek your wellbeing but your gifts. Few, if any are concerned that you get no rest. They push you into the night, through the night and into days until you give them rest; until they get their solution.

This is the reality of ministry, that even while you give yourself to work you have to force yourself to rest. While you give yourself to people, you will have to force yourself away from them, just to catch your breath. That is, if you manifest what they need.

On this dusty afternoon, the man in the center of the mob wiped the sweat from His brow. He was physically exhausted.

He traveled with protocol but at times they could do little when the crowd was pressing in. This minister understood what it meant to be pushed, to feel the heat in the middle all the time with little ventilation; to be mistreated by people seeking just to touch Him. Love and passion kept Him going. His disciples too were exhausted every day trying to protect Him.

"I don't understand how He does it," a lawyer was overheard saying. "The people come to us in the temple and bow down to us on the streets; He goes to the people in the streets and literally bows to their demands; He serves them."

"He is different," another interjected. "Yet, we are no better than everyone else, we go to Him to hear His wisdom and secretly for answers and solutions. I have done it and you have too. Many of us have done it."

"The lawyer laughed; recently the centurion from Capernaum sent a delegation of us to get answers for his sick servant. Such a contradiction to do openly but he built us a synagogue. This was the least we could do for him."

"We live a contradiction and you know it," his companion responded.

One of the persons who followed Jesus heard about the conversation and commented, "Ministry without a mindset of work is mental retardation."

~ ~ ~ ~ ~ ~ ~ ~ ~ ~ ~ ~ ~

This particular evening, Jesus was walking to the house of Jairus. This leader and a ruler of the synagogue had received a report that his daughter was dead and he came and begged Jesus. Previously, the thought of a dead person coming back to life was ridiculous. The ministry of this Man changed all that. Many were now believers and beneficiaries. They were willing to extend themselves for far more than they would previously. To believe the impossible, or rather, to believe that nothing is impossible with Jesus. Jesus had brought such a measure of hope to everyone. He transmitted compassion, love and such care that made them feel secure in the knowledge that He would certainly reward everyone who seeks Him diligently. He was so exalted in His actions yet so reachable, so touchable, so approachable. He would listen and respond even when He was so busy...

This man had faith in the heart of Jesus not just in His ability. Unlike the multitude who came to Him with their problems, this man needed Jesus to come with him to his problem.

Ministry involves a willingness to go, to meet the needs of people in their place of need; to step out of your comfort to bring the comfort of Christ to men; to drop your busy agenda for just one as much as for a multitude. This may sound like a great demand, but indeed, the kingdom is not passive; it is a call to work.

When a kingdom or a nation is at war, every citizen is at war, they all have a war-readiness, fighting mindset. From the days of John the Baptist until now, the kingdom of God suffers violence and it makes every kingdom citizen a force, or rather, a soldier at war.

Throughout the ministry of Jesus, He executed His ministry like someone having to fight to fulfill what He carried, if that adequately described His passion. He was like a man on a mission that did not understand the word pause. Work to Him was the wheels on which the car of His ministry was carried. It was the engine of fulfillment. He knew He would have so much to offer but so little to give without the mindset of work.

Here He was. The crowd was pressing Him. Selfishly, yet unintentionally, abusing Him. None using their conscience to give Him room or space. They would hardly listen to His disciples' attempt to bring order.

In the midst of this chaos, there was a woman. She had an issue of blood that made her unclean. She did not belong among this holy people. Touching her made them unclean. There was no way to get to Jesus without touching them, moving them away, pushing through them; fighting her way to the center where He was, fighting His way to helping them.

There was something about this Jesus that gave the hope and expectation that He could solve her problem. There was something about this Jesus that made her feel He would not embarrass her.

There was something about this Jesus that made her feel that He could touch her touching Him.

"If only I can just touch." Many had reported healing after touching Him. They were pressing on Him as if He was the finish line and all they needed to do was to touch Him, to draw from Him. While many love to be the center of attraction, no one wants to be the center of a mob, all wanting to touch you. This was the reality of the radical ministry of Jesus.

The real situation with the crowd was revealed by the disciples when Jesus turned and said, "Who touched Me?"

When everyone denied it Peter and those with Him said, "Master, the multitudes throng and press You, and You say, 'Who touched Me?'"

The word throng means, crowd, mob and swarm; press means intense contact that applies pressure; painful crushing that may leave bodily injury. This was the reality of the ministry conditions of Jesus. There is no work in the natural that does not require assertion and in many cases pain. Work is punishing to the flesh but the only vehicle to fulfillment.

Jesus acknowledged the healed woman and continued to Jairus' house. Jairus did not provide transportation. There were no motors in those days and although there were donkeys, none was provided. This man of God had to walk. The kingdom mindset refuses to wait on comfort to bring comfort; or stipulate conditions to minister the gifts God has so freely given. It does not demand to be paid in order to pray and reach out. The only currency that moves a kingdom citizen with the heart of the King is compassion.

~ ~ ~ ~ ~ ~ ~ ~ ~ ~ ~ ~

It was another day. The crowd was again so thick that most people could not even see Jesus if they came near. You were especially disadvantaged if you were short.

Again He was on foot, moving and ministering and many followed Him. One man decided that if he was to see Jesus, he would have to climb into a tree. The crowd was too thick and he was too short and diminutive.

Jesus was passing his way but He was not coming alone, in fact, the crowd was so much that you would be aware only that He passed after He passed because the crowd said so. You would not see who had passed. You would not have tapped into what He carried. It too would have passed you unless you became aggressive to press into the crowd or innovative to rise above and beyond the crowd.

His name was Zaccheus, He was a tax collector. Very respected because of his job and hated because the job corrupted its captives. He knew how to get what he wanted, whatever it took.

As he perched in the tree and peered at Jesus from his vantage point, Jesus surprised him and stopped, called him out of his tree and made him the center of His next move. He went to His house and ministered to him. The crowd filled his yard and the surrounding streets as Jesus ministered change. Jesus was very strategic; He had little time but He was determined to make maximum impact.

John quickly turned his Bible to the book of Luke. He wanted to hear what Dr. Luke said about the crowd. He paused at Luke 11:35. It said the crowd was thickly gathered together (NKJV). John's thought was: and Jesus was in the middle with only twelve persons serving as protocol. He moved on to Luke 12:1. It said there was an innumerable multitude of people so they trampled each other. Again, John's thought was: and Jesus was in the middle with only twelve serving protocols.

One person is exertion; a crowd is exhaustion. Having them all the time brings your mother and brothers out calling you mad. John chuckled at his own joke.

So persistent was the crowd that His mother and brothers came to Him but could not get to Him. They wanted to set Him right. Although they had no doubt about His mandate and unique birth, they could not understand His passion and urgency. They could not get to Him. The crowd was too thick. On another occasion, He was in a house and they had to cut through the roof to get a bedridden man to Him because the doorway was completely blocked. All those in the house must have been happy for the ventilation when the roof opened up. Kingdom effectiveness demands sacrifice.

"How do I measure the size of the crowd that came to Jesus," John thought. On one occasion He fed five thousand men plus women and children. On another occasion, he fed three thousand. That would put the crowd above six thousand to over ten thousand on a standard occasion.

The thought of this amount of people without proper crowd management made John kneel in realization and acknowledgment of what Jesus went through to minister. Jesus continued to minister, to teach and to impart. John was further mesmerized when He thought of the nature of the meetings. All included solid teachings but some were deliverance-based.

John could not conceptualize a deliverance meeting with that measure of attendance meant for Jesus. On one occasion it said they brought all the sick and diseased and other needs to Him and He healed them all, excluding none. Furthermore, people were telling everyone that all they needed to do was to touch Him and be healed. They were not just satisfied to listen from a distance. It is safe to say they trampled each other trying to touch him; this was Luke's account.

John paused to reflect on a powerful and cutting edge Nigerian prophet explaining why he had security with guns. He explained that in his early ministry, there was an incident where people were telling others in a particular gathering that he had the anointing, all they needed to do was to connect. He recalled that he was slapped in his head and all over his body by good-intentioned people saying, "I connect, I connect."

He fell to the ground and they were on top of him. No one cared about his well-being, all they wanted to do was to connect. When they were finished, he was left battered and in pain.

Jesus was the subject of the touching ministry also, yet Jesus kept going and was never discouraged.

John reflected on what His family thought about the way He sold Himself to the work. John laughed at the thought as he saw them, ready to hold Him back. They wanted to take Him home and put Him on sedatives. John laughed again as He could hear them say to themselves, "He is mad; He is beside Himself; He is loco; He has gone off a curve!"

That was the statement of the intensity of His ministry. He did not come to be served but to serve. A slave never determines his rest; the job and his master does. Unprofitable servants indeed. God gives us rest or rather is preparing our rest. But while it is day...work!

NO REST

THE PRIVACY OF PUBLIC MINISTRY

John returned to his poem capturing the work ethics of Jesus. He examined the second stanza.

When He sought a private moment, they sought Him
No rest for Him around

~ ~ ~ ~ ~ ~ ~ ~ ~ ~ ~ ~ ~ ~

He could see Him tired, in the hot sun, His foot dusty in His sandals, sweat pouring on His body and drying up, yet He still persisted.

John could see people all around Him. It was a lonely place but they followed Him there on foot. They came for the teaching and were so enthralled that they forgot all about their well-being. They had come great distances without food. They stayed for three days just feeding on His word. They ignored the fact that they would be out of options for food and be extremely hungry. There was a hunger in them for what Jesus was serving that took them beyond the physical doctrine of their rumbling stomachs.

Jesus had resorted to the mountainside after hearing how John was slaughtered like an ordinary animal and his head served on a platter to satisfy the vindictive hunger of a wicked woman. If rest, retreat and meditation time is what He desired, this would not be granted. Ministry can be brutal, especially when the people recognize the need for what you carry.

If He wanted a break, the multitude would offer none. He had compassion on them and He taught them as a shepherd would. After this, He saw the multitude and recognized they were in dire need. He knew how hungry they must have been there in the desert. He forgot His own needs and the painful loss of John and focused on them. After teaching them dedicatedly Jesus said to His disciples, "Give them something to eat."

"Indeed, it is amazing," John thought. "If these people came so far and they were with Jesus so long, what does it say about Jesus Himself who ministered to them constantly?"

Certainly, He Himself was tired and hungry. He must have been very exhausted physically, perhaps strengthened only by that spiritual wind; the flow of spiritual adrenaline that makes you rise above physical limits. The food you eat that others do not know about, just as He said to His disciples at the well of Samaria. He had been feeding them with the word for so long. They had not eaten food because for three days He was passionately teaching and they were enthralled and engaged. They were not complaining. There is a place with the word and in the presence of God where food becomes secondary. The need only hits you when you step away from the presence. Though they did not assert themselves, they were tired and He knew it.

Jesus, through His hunger and exhaustion, thought about the multitude and could not let it slip? The disciples wanted to send them away but that was never His intention. The heart of the Master was to feed them despite His own infirmities and weakness.

Ministry will always take you beyond self to meet the needs of the people. The believers' life calls them to honor, and to give preference to each other. It requires us to love others as we love ourselves which commits us to give preference to others. Ministry is self-sacrifice. Living like Christ is work.

Following Jesus requires more than just following Him to the cross to seek forgiveness, it is actually taking up the cross and following Him, until the cross takes us up completely, as it took Him up.

It is a lifestyle of work and sacrifice for others. It is seeking out and meeting needs rather than seeking to have our needs met while others are kept out.

CONQUEST OR COMFORT?

KINGDOM DEMANDS CONQUEST

John then sought to further answer the questions he had asked in the poem before:

Was he ever in the comfort
Of a home and a cozy bed to sleep?
Did he ever have a place to lay his head?

"Master, where are we going today?" John could hear a disciple asking Jesus.

"We are going to Capernaum," He replied.

This was a rare occasion since they were prepared to just follow. At times he would take the ministry to His designation but at times the ministry would take Him. So many things would happen in one day as they traveled the dusty roads.

Following Jesus was never easy. As Jesus would say, "The disciple is not above his master." Everything Jesus encountered they encountered. They experienced hunger many times. They had to manage the crowd seeking to mob their master. At times they were manhandled by the crowd. They were committed. They were the protocols that facilitated the manifestation of the anointing they followed. They endured the insults on their Master, most of the time restrained by Him. Two of the disciples once offered Jesus to call down fire from heaven in response to rejection. And they suffered as He suffered in the hands of the Jews as they saw their hope crucified on the cross.

The multitude followed Jesus everywhere. They were persistent. They came out for the signs and for the miracles and He took His time to give them the word of life. They would not readily leave when He was finished. Some lingered. They pushed him beyond human capacity but He kept going. John could see him teaching, loving, reaching, blessing and it attracted people to Him. His disciples were there, but they could do little to keep the pressing crowd from Him. Jesus ministered beyond exhaustion.

One day a man came to Him and said "Master, I will follow you wherever you go."
Jesus replied, "The foxes have holes, and the birds of the air have nests but the Son of Man has no place to lay His head".
Jesus did not go out with the expectation that He would come back to a home, a meal prepared and to a warm comforting bed. He had no expectation of soft, warm and cozy at the end of the day like some of our pastors today. The comfort that warmed His heart daily was doing His Father's will and putting joy in the hearts of men. Sleep was an enemy to His praying culture. It was a robber of time, but He surrendered to its onslaught when He was too tired to resist. He

had no patience with the flesh. He would never live to entertain it.

He was always on the go. He slept on the go, ate on the go and ministered on the go. He lived His mission, was consumed by His mission and radiated His mission. The kingdom was so pressing, His mission so demanding that He kept going constantly.

Jesus recognized that the flesh was given to Him as a vehicle to fulfill His mission. To deliver the spiritual cargo He was carrying. While the vehicle must be maintained, the day it takes precedence over the cargo is the day the mission is stunted. The devil focuses on the flesh so He can divert attention from what we carry. The flesh and its works has to be mortified for the mission to come alive. There is so much more the vehicle can deliver if it is used at maximum efficiency to manage its assignment. Where the focus shifts to the vehicle it becomes a monument instead of a movement; an idol instead of an impact.

John began to sift through some poems he had written to put the flesh in perspective:

> The flesh is a tool
> But that is the heart of it
> We have it to use to live
> But not to bask in it
> We can't do war in it; or walk in it
> Give room to the lust of it
> It has its place
> But is not the benefit

Resist the allure of it
The control of it
It's not the form, beauty or charm of it
But who lives in it
The Spirit of God in you

Flesh is a building, just a temple
So God can have use of it
There's no defense in it
No confidence in it
If you make sense of this
Then you will see
Flesh will damage your gift
It can't dictate or decide
Your effectiveness

John liked this, but he wanted to go through
some others:

For we are the circumcision
Not by knife or by incision
But by Holy Ghost precision
And we have made this decision
To worship God in the Spirit
And not by feelings
No, no, no, not by flesh
We rejoice in Christ Jesus
So flesh be silent
Our vote for you is no confidence
For you can never lead us
Or dictate our impetus
For you won't be our focus

We have no confidence in you

It is a no good thing
In it dwells no good thing
Why should it dictate then
My response to the King
Who in the flesh condemned sin?
We don't owe the flesh a thing
So by its orders, we won't live

So I am gonna, I am gonna use it
Try my best yet one day I'm gonna lose it
Futile are all works that are performed through it
For where I'm going flesh and blood cannot inherit

John liked that too but he reached for another:
The flesh is just a ride
Don't celebrate it
Your confidence is high
But not in its ratings
It's important for it carries in it
All this greatness (you)
It seeks to lead on
To be the definition
Call for a revision
The word is your vision
Tell it, you won't accept that lie

Can't keep it to yourself
Got to display your gifts
So the flesh got to work
And to obey your wish

Release energy from within
For your to do list

Tell it you've got things to do
And flesh you got to go
For people got to know
Now bless the Lord for all His benefits
I command you O my soul

John could picture the fight many have with the flesh when they have to get up at night and pray. Some pray lazily as a concession but there are others who will deny the flesh and pray animatedly for long hours. He wrote:

The flesh is our vehicle
Deny it rest to pray
Throughout the midnight hours
Animated all the way
Summon all its energy
Refuse to let it have a say
It won't die if

WORKING THE WORK

WATCHING THE WORK, WORK WONDERS

John liked the result of this research so much, he added another verse to his poem:

Was He ever without compassion
Wanting to help someone?
Was there ever a moment
Where the hurting could not come?
Was there ever a time He did not
Want to give Himself?
Did He not soar upon the winds of love
By which He was propelled?

John continued writing, this time a partial response:

When He spoke about work
It was as if He was duty bound
I must work My Father's work
Before the sun goes down
I must go to the next town also
No time for a human crown
This kingdom is the reason I am living
For this purpose, I was born

What did Jesus say about His work? The words echoed in John's ears and confirmed everything He studied so far, "I must work the work of Him who sent me while it is day. The night is coming when no one can work."

"Day!" John thought. "What could day mean?"

Certainly, it meant while the opportunity exists; while there is time; while you are alive. The fact that He says the night comes, suggests immediacy of action; urgency; passion for the now. The night then must refer to any intervening circumstance that cuts off opportunity to work; death, sickness, change in location, resources and eventually the end of time.

In other words,

Keep working with what you have,
At every opportunity you have
For opportunity lost may have a forever cost.

The day for Jesus started at the age of thirty when His ministry started; it ended on the cross. That was where our day (empowerment and mandate for ministry) started. It ends when He returns or when our life ends.

"Working the work," John thought. Does that mean the work must be worked otherwise it is just wasted potential and opportunities? How many lives are lost because the work is talked about extensively but not worked; not pursued intently and intentionally? How many people are not delivered, sick, hurting because the work is appreciated but not embraced?

The work is the field white, ready for harvest. Working the work is the engagement of reapers.

> The work is potential
> Great possibility to yield
> But what good is possibilities
> Unless it is received
> Even so the abundance
> Of fruits in the master's field
> Yes, the work; it is of no worth
> Unless it is worked, gathered, reaped

What did Jesus say to the Pharisees, "My Father is working and I work; I only do what I see my Father do."
This entered into one of the biggest contradiction of their faith, yet they ignored it to focus on the fact that He called God Father. The contradiction is that God had not ceased working. The presence of the Devil in the earth means there will be work until he rests in his lake of fire.

Paul captured this also. He said if Joshua had given rest, he would have spoken of another day. Let us labor to enter into rest, for the night comes when labor ends and rest starts.

John then concluded: as long as the devil is active, the mindset of war and the mindset of work remains; winning requires force and violence. From the days of John until now, the kingdom suffers violence and believers are called to war, to take it forcefully, violently.
War means assertion, aggression, exertion, sweat and blood.

SHARPENING THE AX

JESUS MINISTERED TO HIS DISCIPLES

Those who waters must be watered
In word and in prayer
So their effectiveness is not watered down
And they maintain the fire
Like an ax, the more you are used
The greater is the need
To re-sharpen your tool
So your impact won't recede
Keep the prayer burning
So the fire is not quenched
For if your ax is dull
You expend foolish strength

John could see Him; he could see Jesus, he could see His disciples, a bunch that kept going like ministry machines wired with flesh. They were tired and exhausted most of the time. They had little time to sleep or rest. On a normal day, Jesus had exhausted His day teaching and ministering to needs. His day would many times engage the heat of the sun and go into the night. Yet after all this, He took the time to explain everything to His disciples, well into the night. After this, He would pray the night away. How did He do it?

The kingdom mindset of work never ignores the ax. If the ax is dull the work gets harder with less impact and lower results in the end. Jesus is the Word. He poured Himself into His disciples. He ensured they not only spend time serving Him, but they spent time with Him. This strategy became so obvious to the world that after His death they observed the boldness of Peter and John. They knew they were uneducated so their confidence and answers amazed them. They befuddled the lawyers and Pharisees. They searched for answers and they came to one conclusion. They had been with the Lord.

Jesus poured Himself into them personally then after He was finished He took time away by Himself. He spent time in the presence of God for God to pour Himself into Him. He ensured His vision of God; His spiritual eyes and Spiritual ears were fully in tune. The ax is a tool for work, but it needs to spend time with the owner to be sharpened. For if the ax is dull...

Ecclesiastes 10:10 If the ax is dull, and one does not sharpen it, he must use more strength. Wisdom brings success.

MINISTRY IS FOOD-FILLING

MORE THAN MY NECESSARY FOOD

A hungry man without food
Is on involuntary fast
But when food is available
He runs to get it fast
When ministry attracts you more
And food loses its allure
So the hungry man ignores
His stomach crying as before
You know that to eyes that will see Him
And hearts that will obey
God's will is more food-filling
Than a mouthful any day

John could see Him exhausted, tired after a long walk. They reached Samaria and stopped at the well on the outskirts. His disciples had left Him to get food. They were hungry as at many other times. Ministry does not guarantee comfort, but it is your guarantee of fulfilment and joy if you find impact comforting.

Jesus sat at the well waiting for His disciples to return. As He waited a woman came to the well to draw water. It was an unusual time. It was obvious she preferred solitude. Was there something unusual about her why she did not fit in? Jesus was very hungry but he saw in her a ministry opportunity He would not readily let go of. It is so easy to be distracted from ministry by personal needs. It is so easy to allow feelings to interfere with doing His pleasing. When we surrender to the temptation to please ourselves first, to put our needs before ministry, it becomes obvious that the kingdom is not our priority. We are instructed to seek the kingdom and all its righteousness first and let God handle our case.

The disciples returned and saw Him talking to the woman. They were surprised. She did not fit the ministry profile. She seemed to be impacted and enthusiastic as she hurried away. "Woman, your water pots..."
She was gone; she simply left them there.
There was a renewed energy with their master also. Something that only ministry ignited. Well, they knew something about Him. He was hungry, very hungry. They all were. They had come a long way on foot and had not eaten for some time.
They brought the food to Him and said, "Master, eat."
He was not interested. This baffled them. "Master, we went and bought you food. You are very hungry, eat."
Again He refused. This time He responded, "I have food to eat that you do not know about."

They did not recognize how much the work rejuvenated Him; how much doing God's will was more fulfilling that the filling of the stomach. That is why believers fast, and ministers who are very serious about impact eat nothing before ministry. The kingdom mindset of work puts impact above intake; kingdom expansion above self-preservation. The body is the tool to achieve the objectives of the Spirit. At times we choose to keep the body empty and the Spirit full so it does not interfere with ministry; especially when you are ministering to a prostitute or to controversial people like the Samaritans.

They could not understand so they began to ask among themselves, "Who gave Him food to eat?"

They knew the attitude of work and the execution many times saw them working on empty stomachs. Once they passed through a cornfield and helped themselves. Cooking the corn in their hands with a rub before they ate it raw. Many times the work of the gospel took them into the place of total selflessness and self-sacrifice which exhausted hunger. This was another such time. They had gone to buy food and had returned with it. Jesus was where they left Him with no food option available to Him. His explanation stunned them. He had a ready hoard of food open and fills Him every time He ministers and follows God's instructions. In His response to their bewilderment, He said it plainly, "My food is to do the will of the Father who sent me and to accomplish it."

Jesus was not concerned so much about food-filling as He was about what was full-filling. The work meant more to Him than anything. Food could wait; kingdom was calling. Kingdom first.

He was hungry, extremely hungry, but not for food, for something else... for lost souls. Only work could feed Him in that moment. He fed on work. He fed on doing what the King demanded. The kingdom mind-set of work requires us to feed on the work of the King; to make it our food and everything else. We to eat to live and not live to eat. Ministry is life and all about lives.

~ ~ ~ ~ ~ ~ ~ ~ ~ ~ ~ ~ ~

John could see Him in the house. Martha was busy serving and they were hungry, very hungry, Mary sat at His feet. Martha came to Jesus and said, "Don't you care that my sister is leaving me alone to serve?"
The response of Jesus to her is summarized in four statements:
1. Martha, Martha, you are anxious and worried about many things.
2. One thing is needed.
3. Mary has chosen the better thing.
4. That will not be taken from her.

Life and ministry to the flesh is a full-time job. It comes with the cares of this world and anxiety. It exposes your consciousness about others and comparison with them and what they do. It makes you constantly dissatisfied as you push for perfection in the flesh and angry with your own self for working too little and for working too much. It makes you angry and even insolent with the same person you are trying to serve. A good act is not necessarily a good heart.

The flesh takes you into many things that confuses the call of your spirit. It makes you so busy that you miss the presence even when it is very tangible. It gets you so overworked serving the body that you miss the person of Christ. There is however, one thing needed. That one thing silences the voices of the flesh and puts life into perspective. You can't feed when you need feeding, you will get fed-up with anything. Getting fed-up is a manifestation of what you are feeding. It is a fruit of the flesh.

That one thing overrides every agenda of the flesh and aligns the flesh with the Word.

Mary chose to sit at the feet of Jesus. To bask in His presence. To have Him break the bread of life to her. To sit at the feet of the word and let it flow into the heart. To hug the revelations. To worship the Lord in the beauty of His holiness. Jesus called it the better part. It is the one thing in the midst of the many things that engenders life.

Jesus said that this would not be taken from her. Life throws out many things to us, many distractions. We grab our portion, grapple at times for it. There are many who will be dissatisfied with their portion in life and will fight for yours. It is contradictory for life never forces you, it gives you choices. Mary had chosen and Martha had chosen. Yes, there will be people at all strata of society enjoying contrasting benefits and most times it is a matter of choice at critical points in life, sometimes as early as preparatory education. Our impact in life is also a matter of choice. Do we feed the flesh or feed the spirit? Do we pursue the direction of God or the dictates of the flesh? Do we surrender to its cry of laziness or do we engage the passion of the Spirit and compel the flesh to cooperate? There is one thing you can be sure of, when life rages at you because you defy the flesh and the standards of life; you have the backing of heaven. Heaven will not take it from you and will defend you from those who will be incited by your passion for presence and the work of God. The kingdom mindset of work has the full backing of heaven.

Jesus also had to make a decision as many ministers do. Would He be distracted by His hunger and the cry of the flesh to defend those who are catering for His comfort even above those responding to His ministry?.
There are many in church given privileged places and positions:

> Who are rich and perverted,
> Who bankrolls but are not converted,
> Who will pay the price for their salvation
> and ignore the crucified Christ who died to save them
> Who works for Christ with all passion
> But it is just a supposition
> For they won't let Christ work for them
> and in them;
> Who use effort to keep their place,
> But ignore the effect of grace.
> But they should know that at their best
> It's not by works of righteousness

For Jesus, he would not compromise or show partiality. Not for a minute would He elevate the need of the flesh above the need of the spirit. Not for a minute would He elevate what they are carrying above what He is carrying. They are serving Him because of what He is caring anyway. Ministries fail, but they only fail, when flesh is elevated above spirit. One area of compromise is an entry point for demons of compromise. The kingdom of mindset of work closes the door.

For Jesus, what Martha was doing was food-filling; what Mary was doing was full-filling. Ministry is not fulfilling when you pour out but when people receive and respond adequately to what you pour out. Any true minister will gladly ignore their need to feed those hungry for God. They will gladly ignore the gift of the giver, however needed, to feed the soul of the giver. They would never take away a person's hunger for God, and divert them to serve their hungry flesh, whether materially, carnally or just a meal. The flesh has its place but not as a master but a servant. Every true believer will starve the flesh so the spirit can feed on the word and the will of God. Unless the flesh is restrained believers will never be free to release themselves fully to the word and work of ministry.

Jesus made a very selfless response that ignored his own physical need and comfort. Yes, He was hungry but Mary was hungry for the kingdom, hungry for the word.

You can imagine what Martha must have been thinking, "This is about You Jesus; You are hungry, I know it. Your disciples said it themselves. You haven't eaten for a while. You have been ministering all day. I am doing so much for You and you don't care... You are ignoring me and I am doing everything. You don't care...?"

Truly, Jesus did not care for her cares but for God's care, her soul.

~ ~ ~ ~ ~ ~ ~ ~ ~ ~ ~ ~ ~ ~

John, just thinking about Jesus, recognized how selfish he himself was to entertain the thought of giving up, even momentarily, to feel exhausted and to want to not go on because his father had died. When he thought about the sacrifice of Jesus, it all came together and he felt he was in a good place. He had seen the sacrifice of his father many times but now the thought of Jesus and his meditation on all that Jesus represented and all He did, strengthened John. It took his focus from himself to the people that needed to be reached. He could see the millions who needed to be impressed with this kingdom mind-set of work so they may be effective in their mandate. He could see the many who have received the treasure of the kingdom, the Holy Spirit, but it is not benefiting them because they have not applied the attitude of work Solomon applied. He could see the many who has equal access to the promises of God, all of them but have not accessed them because they have not applied themselves as with every person who has ever achieved anything for the King. He could see the million around the world whose prayers are never answered because they have not adopted the warrior mentality to take the kingdom by force. They ignore the demonic opposition actively working day and night to ensure they never manifest. Daniel fought for twenty-one days and nights until he had an answer to just one prayer. Everyone who will join the well-done club of good and faithful servants; those whom the King will be proud of and will place in His joy, must be prepared to sweat their vision and prayers.

John reflected on Jesus and His work attitude and He had a flash back. He saw Him, he saw Jesus ministering to a multitude and this man called Him and said "My daughter is sick; will you come?" Jesus left the multitude and began to walk to minister to that one person.
What type of heart did He have?"
Who is this Jesus?
Can God be so easily touched and reached?
What manner of compassion is this?
John sat for a while amazed. He was amazed at the extent of the Master's willingness to action His conviction with work?

UNENDING MINISTRY

MINISTERING TO DEATH OR
RATHER TO THE DEPTH BEYOND

Did He ever take vacation?
Did He retire in the end?
Or did He display the manner of love
That makes one die for His friends?
Did the pain of the cross
Cause Him to break His urgency?
Or did this tortured Minister in the midst of pain,
reach out to the thief and all those in need of His ministry?

Unending ministry
Ministers to the end
Undying ministry
Ministers to death, through death
And beyond as it lets go of the flesh
For ministry is spirit
And spirit never dies
We minister in the spirit, of the Spirit
With the word that is spirit
So flesh has no voice
Even when it is crying
Pained and is dying
Ministry is choice

The words of Jesus echoed in His thoughts again, "I must work, the work of Him who sent me while it is day."

John could see the Lamb on the cross. His day was about to end.

For Jesus, the day ended on Calvary.

John was amazed at his own thoughts. He could see Jesus, hanging there on the tree exhausted. The blood on His back, the crown of thorns piercing His head, the people mocking Him. They were loud and distasteful. He focused away from Himself and paid attention to His mother. He wanted to ensure she had trusted care. He committed her to His disciple John. He then prayed for the multitude, that God would forgive them, even in the midst of everything that they were doing to Him. He understood that they did not recognize the spiritual significance of what they were doing. He looked beyond their grueling punishment, intentional torture and mockery. It pained deeply, body, heart and soul. It broke His heart in today's currency, yet He prayed for their forgiveness. He could not have done this if He was listening to His flesh. The pain screamed at Him compelling Him to use His spiritual access to angels to save and avenge it. He refused. The flesh was expendable; the mission was not.

Then the thief on the cross reached out to Him. He was justly crucified for his offense. His flesh screamed at Him from head to toe with pain so excruciating that it made it impossible to hear another person's plea in the moment. He heard it with such clarity as if it was the only thing happening. It made His spirit dance with joy that someone was responding to His sacrifice even before it was complete. This was the purpose of His death. He reached out and hugged the remorse of this condemned thief with great compassion in the midst of His own pain. He, Himself could not physically move, He was nailed, yet He hugged him in the most passionate way. "You will be with me in paradise today," He responded; pain filling his voice adding flavor and a unique glow to the love He demonstrated. In that moment He acknowledged the cry of repentance and sealed His first blood-washed convert.

What message does it send us? Even in pain we minister. Pain or personal problems are no excuses to recoil from ministering. We cannot ignore the field white and ready with so many potential crops spoiling, dying without being reaped, because we are under fire or sinking in our own mire. Our quickest way to the top is helping others up. The sweetest taste of victory is to allow others to rise on your back to theirs. To become that seed that falls and dies so it multiplies and promulgates.

Jesus ministered to His very last breath. He ministered with His very last strength. He ministered as His life ebbed away. The kingdom mind-set of work demands that once you are alive, your mission is your priority. It always takes precedence to your circumstance, feeling and physical capacity.

Jesus had deposited Himself in His disciples while He was with them, now He was willing to die to extend Himself and His passion. Did He not say, "Unless a grain of wheat falls to the ground and die, it abides alone? He was not willing to abide alone. This had nothing to do with salvation since He had no need of salvation; it had everything to do with harvesters, soul-winning; about laborers for the whitened field. The principle of succession demanded that He deposited Himself in millions so that we could not just learn of Him and be saved but that we could become trees of righteousness, springing from the same spiritual root that was planted on the cross. That we would walk this earth with the same character, mind-set and attitude towards God and the kingdom. It requires us to have the same attitude towards the King and the same attitude of work until the kingdom reaches and is established in every heart to the ends of the earth. It requires that the word finds us faithful, ready to teach others also. For indeed, the earth shall be filled with the knowledge of the glory of the Lord, just as the waters cover the sea. Presence comes from above; knowledge is spread by people.

What did Paul say to Timothy? "Everything you have heard from me, that, I have taught you, that I have spoken before everyone else, commit to faithful men who are able to teach others also." The kingdom mindset of work demands that the work perpetuates. That while we work we train. Isn't success measured by succession? Did not Jesus send us out to preach, teach and make disciples? Isn't this what daddy did with me to his very last breath?

Anyone who dies with his gift is a colossal failure no matter how successful his life appears. Anyone who holds on to his gift, the secret of kingdom success, because he is afraid others will use it to become successful or even to compete, is a disgrace to heaven's kingdom investment. John could think of a particular studio technician he knows that is an expert at his trade but hates the thought that others may steal his secret and produce gospel music of his quality.

How did Jesus die. Jesus died ministering. He ministered till death. His death was the beginning of His ministry through others. His debt, or rather our debt to Him is the beginning of ours.

John thought of his father. Did he not die ministering? Did he not minister until he died? Did He not deposit a new passion in me, the passion for work, in the midst of his own intense cancerous pain? The tears fell from John's eyes as the raw pain resolved the moment. "Daddy ministered to the very end. He ministered to me." John would sleep on that thought. He needed the night to regain composure.

~ ~ ~ ~ ~ ~ ~ ~ ~ ~ ~ ~ ~ ~

John woke up in the night, more grateful for Jesus than ever before; more appreciative of his mission. He began his summary which he realized was fully resolved in Jesus. There are many today, who have received salvation because of His death but they reject the spirit of work that He displayed through His life. They have not fully embraced everything He represents. They have not pursued the knowledge necessary to pass on to others and the mind-set of work to pass Him on. It is one package, receiving Him and avenging His death. We have to take up our cross and follow Him. We cannot learn of Him and not encounter His passion and love for all men. We cannot encounter His passion and love without becoming an expression of His love. We cannot love Him without loving His. Love is never passive; love gives. Jesus is known as the gift that keeps on giving. Even in death He continued to give and rose again so He could give His life away through us.

He is the light of the world. That makes us light in this world and gives us the responsibility to let our lights shine before men, that they will see us working and they will see the quality of His work in us, with us, through us and glorify God. The mystery of this is that the work can only be seen if it is worked. No one takes a light and hides it under baskets. It must be visual, persistent, pervasive and engaging to serve its purpose.

John repeated to himself, "Yes, I must work the work of Him who commissioned me to work while it is day, for the night is indeed much closer now than ever when no one can work. This is no time to entertain ourselves, there is so much, so much to do; people to impact, seeds to plant, individuals to deposit Christ into.

~ ~ ~ ~ ~ ~ ~ ~ ~ ~ ~ ~ ~

John could see Jesus alive in the flesh, eating from the food many do not know about, but which causes men to ride on spiritual energy above physical hunger. There is a place in God and in His work that is so satisfying and fulfilling it fills the stomach. To be filled is one thing, to be fulfilled is another level. To be fulfilled is the fullness of being filled. It is to be fully filled with the expression of His fullness. To be filled is easy, food can top you up; to be fulfilled, only work on the wings of purpose may suffice.

Moses fed from the presence of God while he was on the mountain for forty days and nights without food. Jesus lived at this place, not by election but by devotion. In the midst of exhaustion, the entire three years of His ministry, He gave Himself completely to people, to the work that He performed to minister to them, and He gave Himself completely to God. He always made time to pray. Ministry did not keep Him away from the midnight hours.

As Jesus has taught us, work is rounded. We labor in His field and labor in His presence. We find His heart to display His love. We labor in His presence to labor in His field. We know Him in order to make Him known.
Jesus said, "I do the works of My Father;" and again, "I speak what I have seen with My Father." Seeing and hearing comes from proximity. The closer you get the bigger He becomes, the clearer His voice and the louder His heartbeat.

The kingdom mind-set of work requires our mind to be set on the King so that we will perform His work, not ours. We will shine His light not ours, so that men will see our work and give Him the glory, not us.

We close with this passage from the CWDS Bible:
PSALMS 92
...**13**Those who are planted in the house of the Lord shall flourish;

in the courts of our God they shall flourish.

14They shall bring forth fruit in their old age,

they shall be fat and flourishing;

15to show that the Lord is upright:

He is my rock,

and there is no unrighteousness in Him;

no, no unrighteousness at all.

QUOTE: *Your prosperity and longevity has everything to do with your location; be planted in the house of the Lord.*

According to the psalmist, you cannot be planted in the house of the Lord and be useless. You will not only be fruitful but you will not consider retirement, just refirement and refinement. If you are in the house and not active and productive, perhaps you are not planted(heart and soul)...and perhaps, just perhaps, you can be picked up and blown away by a random wind.

CONCLUSION

DEFINITION OF WORK: "PROACTIVELY AVENGING THE CROSS"

John could see his father smiling down at him through the clouds. He felt relief and a new wind flowing through him. Energy came to him like never before. He felt the passion to go and to do everything he had discovered.

If he could report to his father one last time he would say. "I have concluded: this is not the time to rest. The devil never rests. The kingdom of darkness never sleeps. Rest, sleep, or rather, too much of it, laziness, are all feelings inspired by the flesh. They are mere distractions. Satan constantly manipulates our flesh with all these feelings to prevent us from being effective. He fully understands the impact of every person giving themselves to God and His work. His effectiveness to divert, delay and distract is based on our failure to pray and spend time in the word. Persistence without Presence is paltry. Presence without persistence is paltry.

It is not the time for respite. It is not the time to get lost in personal pain or personal pleasure or personal entertainment or anything personal.

We are kingdom citizens. We have a mandate. It is never about us. When comfort gets in the way of mandate, we make ourselves bigger than the kingdom. Pain is a part of life; it is punishing but it does not give us reason to part with our mandate or even to pause it for a moment of pity. While we maintain and preserve the vehicle we do not entertain the vehicle or shift our focus to the vehicle. The vehicle, our body, is only relevant in the earth where it facilitates our mission. The cross testifies to this. Where the vehicle, becomes the mission there is a breakdown, or rather, perversion of purpose.

~ ~ ~ ~ ~ ~ ~ ~ ~ ~ ~ ~ ~

John arose with new resolve. He had a message or rather a lesson for his world. He would get it out through his network initially and he would expand his network to give it out. He would reach men and women everywhere through available mediums and his forums and he would inspire them to be what they were created to be in the first place, ambassadors for Christ, to be working, to shake off the laziness and to get fully engaged and involved. This is life; his life from now on. He could no longer see his father. He loved his father but he could see Christ; the only one his father wanted him to see.

A light shone in the room and John felt empowered as if he was being handed a personal mandate that was much bigger than his father's. It was the mandate his father had but which never started with his father but with Christ. His father was just an instrument.

Someone bigger, someone greater wanted believers to know and understand the call to work and be activated. John could feel a presence as he embraced this revelation. He did not count the time. Hours passed, the light faded and he rose up from that encounter after midnight.

"The field is indeed white," he inhaled through his tears and tenderness. "The harvest can be spoilt in the field if the laborers are not prepared to work. People can go to hell because of our failure to work or to be motivated.

The devil and demonic activities are increasing, Christians need to be more vigilant, more ready with a mindset for battle. The kingdom is calling us to work, to get involved, not to give up, not to give in, not to lift our hands from the plow. Wickedness, witchcraft and demonic activities are intensifying. Darkness is covering the earth while the light is hidden. It has found its way into the church and has infiltrated worship and sapped service. This is the time for kingdom people to put away personal selfishness and to embrace the mandate. The heart of a King is crying for laborers; for them to rise with a heart to work and to make Daddy proud; to enter into His joy. It is the call of the field; white ready and perishable calling for laborers. It is the cry of the Father, "Son will you go and work in my field today."

It is the crippling resistance of the church in comfort and with personal agendas, "I will go. Lead me and I will follow. Make me a vessel. Use me Lord!"

Yet they do not go. And the honest reply of the few, "I will not go!"

It is a matter for prayer that Jesus has committed to every believer, "Pray that God will send laborers." For when you have many players and few goers it is a matter that must be subjected to prayer. Prayer will never change God's heart; His desire is that none will be lost. It may however change yours. Intercession is love on its knees. Love acted on consistently will prompt action. When you begin praying for an army it is hard not to volunteer yourself, even for your friends and family. It is a prayer of conscience that if it finds sincerity will compel action.

The heart of a servant says, "I am at Your bidding. I will do whatever it is you want Master." A true servant rocks at the command of the Master; rides at the demands of the Master and runs at His word. The heart of a deceiver does not care about the commitment he makes; he always feels he has the right to change his words even before God. "Help us to be servants, Jesus, true servants," John prayed.

~ ~ ~ ~ ~ ~ ~ ~ ~ ~ ~ ~ ~

John looked at his watch. He had a ministers meeting in two hours. He wanted to spend time praying first. He had already begun to inspire them to embrace the work of ministry and to maximize their effect. He reflected on the words of Johnson Suleman, a cutting-edge Nigerian prophet who has many sons in various capacities in ministry all over the world: pastors,

evangelists, bishops, general overseers with many branch churches. He said, "Any son of mine whom I call between the hour of twelve am and four am and they do not answer the first time, they are not serious."
Real believers cannot be snoring when they should be roaring. We are an army on our knees.

John had already seen changes and growth in many areas since he began to inspire the culture of work in his ministry. His team had also been fired up, sending the message out by all the ministry platforms and avenues. He would continue to inspire ministers through platforms his father had created and those platforms that God would give him. He had added the finishing touches to his book, and had sent out previews by newsletters which had already reached thousands. The comments were overwhelming.

He had already sat with Bible schools to have the book added to their mandatory reading and the topic included in the curriculums. Effectiveness and fulfillment is not based on knowledge but work. Solomon son of David the prophet made this very clear. He never left school.

John would return to begin work on a Bible study series of children's church lessons and a curriculum on the topic: The Kingdom Mindset of Work. He was animated about the subject. He was committed to train the children and to prepare the youths not just to compete but to be conquerors. He had a burden for the next generation. He knew by observation and revelation the darkness successive generations would face. This generation had become increasingly evil and wicked with people and laws challenging God openly. Witchcraft was on every street side. It pained him to know that the world was in an irreversible regression and would only get worse. Each successive generation will have to fight much harder to accept Christ and to maintain their salvation. The devil, by prophecy, gets angrier and more blatant as his time draws nearer. Believes must get bolder, fiercer and more persistent with their faith. We must understand that rest will never be obtained here. This world has no rest. It keeps groaning waiting for redemption. It knows it will be destroyed to make way for a new heavens and a new earth not stained with blood and corrupted by death. We have no comfort in the flesh nor do we comfort the flesh. The flesh is our clothing to facilitate our mission. We confront it, subdue it, mortify it so we may embrace and maximize our mission and the fullness of life in Christ.

In the words of Jesus, we must work the work of our commission while there is day, for night is coming and that is not questionable. It will intervene. In the words of Paul, we are in redemptive mode. We approach the kingdom as citizens who have gotten a late start; like Paul the apostle born out of time, who spent his days as a believer in redemptive mode. Understanding the contribution we have made to this chaotic world ourselves, we work twice as hard as everyone else, both in prayer, in the word and in the field.

John was fired up for the work of ministry and for the ministry of works. This would be the part of his father that would remain with him all his life. It would be a memorialization of his father's hard work while he lived and a memorial of his father's last days with him. It would be the life portrait he would paint daily and display to his father whom he knew was up there shining like the stars in glory, looking down at him. "Daddy will examine my progress daily as he did with my schoolwork in Junior School."
John could feel the burst of his own energy and excitement and feel his father's heartbeat in his.
Yes, I will work in your field today Father. Daddy, I will work in His field. I will not lie as many still do, saying: I will go... Follow, follow I will follow Jesus, anywhere..., anywhere You lead me I will go..., lead me Lord, I will follow..., Lord, I am available to You... I am Yours Lord, completely Yours...; but hardly making an effort. I will love God as you did and as He commanded, with all my strength, with all my mind, with all my heart; which encompasses all my time and resources.

As the sun sank and disappeared into the night John smiled, "I will never allow the Son to disappear into the night; into this world of darkness. No, I will work the work of my Father in heaven while there is day. As long as I am in this world I am the light of the world, I bring the Light, Jesus, to my world daily. He must shine and not be lost in this demonic age of darkness. It demands all my energy and time. I will give it. God forbid that I should get distracted by creation, to include this molded masterpiece of clay and ignore the Creator, His intimate kiss of breath that makes me alive and His purpose of my existence. I can't say like the many, "My will not His be done."

Nor can I be like the others that say, "His will not mine.." yet Jesus is saying daily, "why do you call me Lord and refuse to follow my instructions."

My commitment is to make the Creator my life. It demands my energy, my strength, my mind, my everything. To truly love Him. I am convinced it is not how intelligent we are, it is the level of work and discipline we apply ourselves to. It is not what we carry, we all have the same Holy Spirit, it is the level of attention and expression we give to Him.

Until I draw my last breath, yes, until my night comes, I will embrace the mission of the cross, to engage the spirit of the cross and avenge the blood of the cross, by extending the mission of the One who took the death of the cross to embrace this entire world.